A Study of Students at Risk:
Collaborating to Do Research

by
Jack Frymier

Phi Delta Kappa Educational Foundation
Bloomington, Indiana

Cover design by Victoria Voelker

Library of Congress Catalog Card Number 89-63307
ISBN 0-87367-801-X

Coordinating Committee of the Phi Delta Kappa Chapter-Based Research Project

Jack Frymier, Senior Fellow
Phi Delta Kappa International

Larry Barber, Director
Phi Delta Kappa Center on
Evaluation, Research, and
  Development

Ruben Carriedo, Director
Planning, Research, and
  Evaluation
San Diego Public Schools

William Denton, Assistant
  Superintendent
Midland, Texas, Public Schools

Bruce Gansneder, Professor
Bureau of Educational
  Research
University of Virginia

Sharon Johnson-Lewis,
  Director
Evaluation and Testing
Detroit Public Schools

Neville Robertson, Director
Phi Delta Kappa Center for
  the Dissemination of
  Innovative Programs

Preface

Organizations, like individuals, are driven by two basic needs: the need to maintain themselves and the need to improve.

Maintenance requires organizations (and individuals) to do whatever is necessary to ensure their continued existence. Repeating traditional activities generally ensures survival, and survival is the name of the game.

Improvement requires organizations (and individuals) to stretch themselves, to be inventive, to vary the ends they typically pursue or the means they employ. Improvement presumes change.

In 1986 Phi Delta Kappa's Future's Committee challenged the organization to change in *Phi Delta Kappa: 2000 and Beyond*.

> Phi Delta Kappa has a choice. The organization can continue in its present role, providing good programs for good purposes. Or it can change. It can become a great organization. It can be the best. . . .
>
> The problems facing educators and society today are so perplexing, the value conflicts so distressing, the fiscal and other resources so unequally distributed, and the press for improvement so demanding, Phi Delta Kappa must create new and different ways to mobilize its members' energies and the organization's resources to deal with these new realities.
>
> The new problems of a new age require different, better solutions than those of yesterday or even today. Identifying significant new developments and creating effective response mechanisms must become the norm if Phi Delta Kappa is to stay out front, on the "cutting edge." (pp. 2-3)

"Mobilizing its members' energies" and "creating new response mechanisms" are what this monograph is all about. This is the story of a professional organization at work. The organization is Phi Delta Kappa. The work is research.

This story shows how a professional organization used its chapter network structure and membership to accomplish research. The story also shows that, if the research is conceptualized appropriately from the outset, new research strategies can be tried and tested in the process.

Using an organization to do research is not a new idea. Using the framework of an organization to conduct identical research in various locations simultaneously is a new dimension for organizational activity.

After the Future's Committee report was issued in 1986, Phi Delta Kappa initiated many improvement efforts by upgrading services, issuing new publications, disseminating new programs, expanding program opportunities for both members and chapters, and sponsoring more Professional Development Institutes, to name a few. This report recounts the story of one improvement venture that was conceptualized, conducted, and completed by Phi Delta Kappa members working with and through their chapters in 87 communities throughout the United States and Canada.

The project described in this monograph focused on two of the five areas singled out by the Future's Committee for special emphasis: 1) school and professional improvement and 2) education research.

Regarding school and professional improvement, the Future's Report argued that "educators who expect to become more capable professionals and to develop better institutions need knowledge and relevant information to help them deal with the problems they face each working day" (p. 6). The report continued:

> Professionals must also have opportunities to develop appropriate professional skills: to try things out; to test ideas against reality; to experiment. . . .
> But even knowledge, understanding, and skill are insufficient. Commitment and dedication are also required. Commitment to the basic purpose of Phi Delta Kappa: promoting quality education. And dedication to the service ethic: helping other people. Professionalism, as a concept, is rooted in the notion of serving others. (p. 7)

Urging members to live up to "the ideal of high quality leadership through research, teaching, and other professional services," the Future's Report emphasized research as "the underpinning of every real profession." Research results in the creation of new knowledge that "can lead to understanding, and understanding is the bedrock on which professional decisions must be made" (p. 13).

The report emphasized that "Phi Delta Kappa must devise ways to encourage and facilitate research by individual members and by chapters." Toward that end, various possibilities were suggested. One of those suggestions is described below:

> Sponsor a different research project every biennium in which Phi Delta Kappa International and local chapters would collaborate. Identify an important area to be studied. Issue a Request for Proposals (RFP). Contract with a Senior Fellow to accomplish a cooperative research project that would deliberately involve local chapters that choose to participate. Repeat the process every two years on a different topic, with a different scholar, and with different chapters. (p. 14)

A Study of Students at Risk: Collaborating to Do Research is one of the organization's responses to the challenges set forth by the Future's Committee. A lot of people — inside and outside of Phi Delta Kappa — were convinced that this project would not "work"; that it could not be done. But it did work, and it did get done. And it worked for several reasons.

First, the project addressed an important problem area. Second, people volunteered their time and their abilities. Third, the organizational routines expedited such needs as communication, materials, and transportation. Fourth, Kappans value inquiry. Fifth, the training manual clarified and standardized procedures. Sixth, the training of leaders from every chapter ensured a common understanding of complex realities and generated a spirit of collegiality. And there were other things.

In the chapters that follow, "A Study of Students at Risk" is described. This publication is not the final report of the study. That report will be published in the months ahead.

This monograph reviews the history of the project within Phi Delta Kappa as an organization: how the project got started, how the problem was identified, how the organization mobilized itself to study the problem, how the study was accomplished, an overview of the results, the significance of certain methodological aspects of the study, how various chapters' research committees functioned, how many people participated, what they actually did, and how they felt about what they did.

This is a story consistent with the ideals of Phi Delta Kappa, as stressed to every new member in the initiation ceremony:

> Research is one of our guiding principles. Through research our knowledge increases and the practice of education improves. Without it our profession will neither grow nor flourish.

This is a story of organizational development and organizational change.

Table of Contents

Chapter One
Getting Started

Phi Delta Kappa is a professional organization in education. There are about 139,000 members organized in 659 chapters around the world. Most of the chapters are in the United States. Governance of the organization is vested in a Board of Directors, which meets twice each year, and a Biennial Council with delegates from all chapters, which meets in alternate years. Daily operations are assigned to a professional staff.

Phi Delta Kappa's Constitution describes the basic mission of the organization:

> The purpose of Phi Delta Kappa shall be to promote quality education, with particular emphasis on publicly supported education, as essential to the development and maintenance of a democratic way of life. This purpose shall be accomplished through the genuine acceptance, continuing interpretation, and appropriate implementation of the ideal of high quality leadership through research, teaching, and other professional services concerned with and directed to the improvement of education, especially of publicly supported and universally available education. (Article 1, Section 3)

The commitments are to quality education and public education. But achieving quality in public education has become an issue in recent years. Some people have urged the privatization of public schools. Others have pressed for more testing and accountability. Still others have advocated a narrowing of programs, a return to what schools used to be. Disagreement exists about both the ends and means of public education.

We live in an issue-oriented age, and issues in education are matters of public concern. The mere existence of critical issues usually means difficulties for professionals. Progress toward agreed-on goals is often stymied. Debate about resource allocations is common. Assumptions are challenged. Motives are questioned.

Committed to the idea of trying to "stay on top" of education issues, Phi Delta Kappa established a special Issues Board in 1986 to identify, monitor, and coordinate the organization's response to developing issues and problems in the field of education. The Issues Board includes the president, president-elect, executive director, editor of the *Kappan*, and senior fellow.

Meeting monthly, or as the occasion demands, Issues Board members try to pinpoint new or emerging issues in education before they become "full blown." Or, if an issue erupts, they may commission an inquiry or establish a work group to study the problem and suggest alternative courses of action. The Issues Board alerts members to new and emerging areas of difficulty and to appropriate courses of professional action.

In keeping with these missions, a list of 14 issues thought to be important to teachers and administrators was developed by the Issues Board during the summer of 1987. An earlier version of the list had been compiled in response to suggestions from each Issues Board member's informal network and that person's general knowledge of the field, but several of the issues on the original list were discarded after surveying officers of Phi Delta Kappa. Others were added from a list developed by the director of Phi Delta Kappa's Center for Evaluation, Development, and Research from an analysis of responses to an open-ended questionnaire by officers in other professional organizations and agencies.

Finally, the Issues Board decided to survey the delegates at the 41st Biennial Council in Louisville, Kentucky, in October 1987 regarding these issues. Each of the 14 issues was described in about 25 to 30 words. Delegates were asked to indicate "how critical each issue is likely to be by 1990 — for society and for the profession — and how much attention will each issue demand?" Responses were made according to a five-point scale:

A — very critical, will demand a lot of attention.
B — fairly critical, will demand fair amount of attention.

C – average critical, will demand average attention.
D – not very critical, will demand minimal attention.
E – not critical at all, will demand no attention.

In addition to the list of 14 issues, the possibility of a collaborative research project by chapters was described in detail. One paragraph from that description follows:

> Working together, many chapters of Phi Delta Kappa could accomplish a significant study of a significant issue in education. Such a project would require each participating chapter to establish a research team, to undergo a training program, to collect data, and to transmit those data to a coordinating committee by the dates specified.

After reading the statement above, delegates were asked to respond to one additional question: "Do you think your chapter would be interested in participating in such a project?"

A total of 808 usable responses were collected from the delegates. There were 635 chapters represented, each with a delegate and some with alternate delegates. Most of the responses received were from delegates, and obviously some alternates also responded. Because respondents were not asked for their names or chapter numbers (to ensure anonymity), and since some response sheets were discarded because they had not been filled out properly, it could not be determined exactly how many chapters participated in the survey. But clearly most of them did.

Responses to each of the 14 issues were summarized for all 808 persons completing the questionnaire. Each response to an issue was accorded a numerical value, depending on how the delegate marked the optical scan answer blank. "A" responses (that is, "very critical") were accorded a value of "5," "B" responses were accorded a value of "4," and so on, down through "E" responses ("not critical at all"), which were accorded a value of "1."

The number of respondents who answered "Yes" or "No" to the question about interest in participating in a collaborative research project were totaled.

Table 1 indicates how 808 Phi Delta Kappa delegates responded to the critical issues questionnaire. Rank order and mean values for each of the 14 issues to which the delegates responded are reported.

In response to the question that asked delegates to indicate the interest of their chapter in participating in a research study of one or

3

Table 1.
Rank Order Listing of Issues Seen as Especially Critical
by the Year 1990
(N = 808)

Rank Order	Issue	Mean Value
1	at risk/neglected/abused students	4.69
2	changing demographic factors	4.36
3	public support and confidence in education	4.34
4	improving the effectiveness of schools	4.33
5	financing public schools	4.16
6	selection and preparation of teachers	4.08
7	attitudes of professionals	4.03
8	AIDS/AIDS testing/fear of AIDS	4.01
9	special problems in urban schools	3.82
10	accountability	3.71
11	evaluating teachers	3.70
12	top-down/mandated reform	3.65
13	court decisions about curriculum content	3.65
14	privatization of public education	3.34

more of the critical issues in education, 646 (80%) said, "Yes, we would be interested"; 77 (9.5%) said, "No, we would not be interested"; and 85 (10.5%) gave no response.

What do these data mean? One interpretation might be that the top four issues were related, statistically and causally, in a significant way. On the questionnaire, what were seen as the two top issues were described this way:

> *At Risk/Neglected/Abused Students:* Children who are low achievers, potential dropouts, pregnant teenagers, latchkey children, or children who suffer from abuse, neglect, drugs, or alcohol.

> *Changing Demographic Factors:* Increasing number of minorities, non-English-speaking families, children born out of wedlock, single-parent homes, elderly, and declining school enrollments with fewer taxpayers as parents.

Research suggests that children who are low achievers, dropouts, or pregnant teenagers are disproportionately children who are minorities or come from non-English-speaking or single-parent families.

4

Many youngsters having difficulty in school were themselves born out of wedlock. They are frequently the same children who suffer most from abuse and neglect or who use drugs or alcohol. The changing demographic situation probably contributes directly to the increase in the number of at-risk/neglected/abused students.

The issues ranked three and four were described on the survey like this:

> *Public Support and Confidence in Education:* Declining support for public schools, importance of public schools in a democracy not understood, help people understand how better schools mean a better economy and a better culture.

> *Improving the Effectiveness of Schools:* Raise students' achievement levels, reduce drop-out rates, improve students' attitudes toward school, help students become more responsible and competent as learners and citizens.

Given the problems outlined in the top two issues, it would seem that improving the effectiveness of schools was seen as the only way to restore public support and confidence in education. In other words, aware of the learning difficulties and other problems that at-risk, neglected, and abused students have as a consequence of the changing demographic situation in America, 808 members of Phi Delta Kappa evidently felt an obligation to improve the effectiveness of public schools so that the confidence and support of the general public can be restored.

The fact that more than 80% of the respondents (probably about 500 chapters) indicated that they thought their chapter would "be interested and willing to participate in a research study involving one or more of these issues" suggested a genuine commitment to deal with the issues head-on, to act, to become involved.

The PDK Constitution states that the basic purpose of Phi Delta Kappa shall be "to promote quality education." "Promote" is an action-oriented verb. It means "to urge the adoption of, to advocate, or to contribute to the progress or growth of." Participating with other chapters in a collaborative research study of the four top-ranked issues was a way to promote quality education that was consistent with Phi Delta Kappa's basic purpose and its traditional commitments to leadership, research, and service.

A proposal was developed to involve chapters of Phi Delta Kappa in a study of students at risk. This proposal was approved by the organization's Board of Directors in January 1988. The board made funds available for up to 100 chapters to collaborate in a research effort. A committee of researchers was appointed in February 1988 to conceptualize and coordinate the study.

The proposal to the Board of Directors outlined a project designed to do two things:

1. generate good data about the four issues described above; and
2. generate enthusiasm, participation, and a sense of accomplishment in research among Phi Delta Kappa members in up to 100 chapters.

It was stipulated that the precise nature of the problem would be developed by a coordinating committee appointed by the president of Phi Delta Kappa and that the intent would be to report to the Biennial Council in October 1989.

On 16 February 1988, a letter was mailed to the president and research representative of every chapter of Phi Delta Kappa, inviting them to apply before April 15 to participate in the project. In mid-March a follow-up notice was mailed to every officer in every chapter in Phi Delta Kappa in a general mailing that included other materials.

Among other things, the original letter of invitation said:

> This letter is an invitation to you and your chapter to join with other chapters of Phi Delta Kappa in a collaborative research project to study the issues that are seen as critical in education.
>
> Last week the Board of Directors funded a proposal for up to 100 chapters to participate in a collaborative research study of critical issues in education. Phi Delta Kappa is now in a position to conduct the study by drawing upon the talents of the members and the resources of the organization.
>
> No other group could accomplish such an undertaking. Phi Delta Kappa can pull it off.

A total of 222 chapters submitted proposals to participate that were postmarked on or before 15 April 1988. In addition, 18 other chapters submitted proposals that were postmarked after that date. In other words, 240 chapters − more than one-third of all chapters in Phi Delta Kappa − expressed interest in being part of this collaborative research effort and submitted a formal proposal requesting participation. In addition, each proposal included a commitment by the chapter to pay up to $300 for hotel and meal costs as part of the obligation of participation.

A committee of Kappans evaluated the proposals. Following a careful review of all proposals in early May, the list was reduced to 106. A committee of Headquarters staff further reduced the number to 100 after considering such factors as geography, costs for transportation, and urban areas represented. On 16 May 1988, 100 chapters were notified of their acceptance into the project and 140 chapters were notified that they were not accepted. The map in Appendix A shows the location of the participating chapters.

In March 1988, a committee of researchers was appointed by the president to coordinate the collaborative research project for Phi Delta Kappa. The following persons agreed to serve:

Ruben Carriedo, director of Planning, Research, and Evaluation for the San Diego Public Schools

William Denton, assistant superintendent, Midland, Texas, Public Schools

Bruce Gansneder, professor, Bureau of Educational Research, University of Virginia

Sharon Johnson-Lewis, director of Evaluation and Testing, Detroit Public Schools

Larry Barber, director, Phi Delta Kappa Center for Evaluation, Development, and Research

Neville Robertson, director, Phi Delta Kappa Center for the Dissemination of Innovative Programs

Jack Frymier, senior fellow, Phi Delta Kappa, chairman

The general assumption, as expressed in the original proposal, was that this research project

> would be a truly collaborative effort between chapters and Headquarters in the sense that the ideas for such a project grew out of the Future's Committee Report (centralized), but the topic to be studied emerged from an analysis of responses of representatives from 635 chapters meeting in session at a Biennial Council (decentralized). The proposal was developed by Headquarters staff (centralized) and would be implemented by a coordinating committee (centralized), but data would be collected in each area (decentralized) and data would be interpreted by representatives of chapters meeting at the district level (decentralized) before a final report was written (centralized). However, each chapter would also be encouraged and assisted in developing special reports and other communications to people within their own locale (decentralized), based upon their own interpreta-

7

tion of their own data in relation to the summarized data for all chapters.

The coordinating committee met three times between March and June 1988 to conceptualize the study, to develop instruments and procedures that chapters would use to collect data, and to plan a training session for chapter representatives.

Four questions were posed to provide direction for the research effort:

1. Who is at risk?
2. What are they like?
3. What is the school doing to help these students?
4. How effective are these efforts?

The theoretical rationale presumed that the student would be the focus of the study, but five factors or sets of conditions impinge on the student and affect the extent to which a student is or is not "at risk": family, peers, school, life events, and community.

The focus was on students, but all data were obtained from professionals by professionals. Student data were obtained from a study of students' records; students were not queried or observed directly, except in the case study.

Although the major focus was on at-riskness among students, data collected from teachers and principals included information about the other issues identified as important by delegates at the Biennial Council: changing demographics, confidence in public education, and school effectiveness.

It was decided at the outset that all data collected would be analyzed two ways: separately for each chapter, and aggregated for all chapters combined.

Chapter Two
Getting the Jobs Done

To answer the four questions posed in Chapter One (Who is at risk? What are they like? What is the school doing? and How effective are those efforts?), a plan was developed for chapters to collect data from schools in their own geographic area using common definitions and uniform procedures established by the coordinating committee.

In effect, each chapter was asked to do various "jobs," each of which involved certain "tasks," which in turn established a time line for completing the study. Each participating chapter was directed to complete these 13 jobs by the date indicated:

1. Form a research committee (1 October 1988).
2. Select three schools in the chapter's area (1 October 1988).
3. Go through extensive training (10 October 1988).
4. Interview the principal in each school (16 December 1988).
5. Survey the teachers in each school (16 December 1988).
6. Apply "Holding Power Statistics" in the high school (16 December 1988).
7. Write a narrative report about each school (16 December 1988).
8. Collect information about students in each school (16 December 1988).
9. Do a case study of one student (1 February 1989).
10. Do at least one optional project (1 February 1989).

11. Do further analyses of data (optional) (1 August 1989).
12. Discuss the data at a district-level meeting (1 May 1989).
13. Disseminate the research results.

Detailed instructions to chapters about the "tasks" required for each job were prepared and published in a *Manual of Instructions* (Frymier et al. 1988). Persons interested in a complete description of the methodology are referred to that document.

Training Participants

On 1 August 1988, descriptions of the first two jobs (that is, "Form a Research Committee" and "Select Three Schools") were mailed to each participating chapter. The local chapter coordinators were directed to form a committee and select three schools before October 1. On 1 September 1988, an airline ticket and the complete *Manual of Instructions* were mailed to each chapter.

During the first week in October, 100 representatives from participating chapters convened in Kansas City for three days of training. Training was conducted by members of the coordinating committee that had conceptualized the study, under the leadership of an outside consultant, Dr. Roy Forbes.

Training sessions consisted primarily of intensive instruction in how to do each job, as detailed in the *Manual of Instructions*. All training took place in small-group settings (less than 15 people), except for clarifying sessions, when the entire group assembled. All of the instructional sessions focused on one job at a time. The person responsible for training participants in a particular job was the person who had responsibility for conceptualizing that portion of the manual.

Following the training, participants returned to their communities and accomplished most of the data collection activities between 10 October and 15 December 1988. The various jobs described in detail in the manual are outlined briefly below.

The 13 Jobs

Job 1, Form a Research Committee: Each chapter formed a research committee before 1 October 1988. To form a local research committee, each chapter was required to accomplish five tasks. The first was an overview of the 13 jobs involved in the project. The second involved instructing the chapter project director to review all of the jobs to be done in order to answer this question: "What kinds of experiences and skills would be most helpful to get these jobs done?" People with strengths in different areas were important. The third and fourth tasks involved identifying Kappans who possessed those kinds of experiences and strengths and asking them to serve. The fifth task required the chapter project director to emphasize to persons invited to help the importance of completing the project.

Job 2, Select Three Schools: Each chapter selected three schools in which to collect data for the study. The selection of schools was accomplished by the local committee acting as a whole. Six tasks were involved in selecting the three schools.

Although chapters were not selected to participate in this project on a random sample basis that was representative of the nation as a whole, they were directed to select three schools that were representative of the geographic area served by the chapter, including one elementary school, one middle school, and one senior high school.

The local committee considered the characteristics of the various school districts that made up the area served by the local chapter: size of districts, number of buildings, age of buildings, nature of programs, number and type of students served, and the age and experience of faculty members. Each chapter considered the traditions, philosophies, leadership, financial support, and other resources available to the schools. They also considered the demographic factors and changes that had occurred in the community in recent years: racial and cultural diversity, economic and social factors, employment opportunities, wages, industries, housing, transportation, communication, government, deterioration in the community, debt, unemployment, morale, degree and nature of racial/ethnic conflict, and the like.

Given these considerations, each chapter made every effort to select three schools that represented the area as a whole. All schools selected were public schools; each school included the grade levels specified; and the schools reflected the cultural factors evident within the general area served by the chapter. Further, no special schools were selected (for example, vocational schools, schools for the gifted).

Job 3, Prepare for the Study: Each chapter selected to participate in the study sent one person to a three-day training session in Kansas City in early October 1988. Transportation was provided by Phi Delta Kappa International, but each chapter paid for the participant's hotel and meal expenses.

11

Following the Kansas City training session, each chapter project director conducted training sessions for the local research committee, using the *Manual of Instructions* as a basis for the training.

Job 4, Interview the Principal of Each School: After the three schools were selected for the study, the local research committee interviewed the principal of each school using a structured interview provided by the coordinating committee. Each principal received a copy of the interview beforehand, so factual information requested could be readily available. The interview involved 159 questions, and each principal and school was assured of absolute anonymity.

Job 5, Survey the Teachers in Each School: Each local research committee made arrangements with the principal about surveying the teachers in that school. Where possible, teachers responded to the survey instrument at a regular meeting of the faculty. If that could not be arranged, they received the survey forms and materials explaining the purpose of the study through the school's mail distribution system. All teachers were asked to participate.

Many of the questions to which teachers responded were identical to questions asked of principals. However, teachers marked their answers on an optical-scan answer blank. There were 100 questions regarding students at risk, plus factual questions about the teachers' age, experience, teaching conditions, and the like. Care was taken to assure teachers that their answers would be anonymous and that their answer blanks would not be collected by the principal.

Job 6, Apply "Holding Power Statistic" in the High School: Each chapter participating in the study collected data in a senior high school, which traced first-time, ninth-grade enrollees for a four-year period, from fall 1984 through spring 1988.

Students who enrolled as ninth-graders for the first time in 1984 were identified by name and ID number, then their official records were examined to identify those who graduated in 1988, those who graduated before 1988, those who requested transcripts be sent to another school, those who went to jail or were institutionalized, those who died and the cause of death, and those who were still enrolled in school.

Using these data, a formula to determine "holding power" was applied. All statistical data were submitted to the coordinating committee.

Job 7, Write a Narrative Report About Each School: Each participating chapter prepared a brief narrative describing each of the three schools in which data were collected. The intent was to generate contextual information that would enable researchers and others to know more about the situations from which the data were derived.

For example, chapters described the school district in which each school was located, including size of the district; number of students, teachers, and buildings, central office operations, traditions, board-administrator relationships, racial composition of population, and the like. In addition, the chapter described specific things about each school: students, teachers, principals, parents, the community, the school's orientation toward students at risk, and its effectiveness in dealing with at-risk students.

Job 8, Collect Information About Students: Each local project director worked with the principal and others to select approximately 100 "typical" students in each of the three area schools selected for the study: 100 fourth-graders, 100 seventh-graders, and 100 tenth-graders. Students assigned to special classrooms or special schools (for example, special education, gifted classes, vocational schools) were not included in the study.

In each school the chapter research team met with teachers and guidance counselors who knew the students best and who worked with them on a daily basis. The teachers and counselors studied each student's cumulative folder and other records carefully, then provided detailed information about each student to the local researchers. The students were identified to the research team only by ID number.

Three types of information were collected about students: demographic, at-risk indicators, and instructional program factors. Birth date, sex, race, and grade level constituted the demographic indicators. The at-risk indicators were 45 factors that previous research suggested contribute to a student being at risk. Each of these 45 indicators was defined operationally, and information was obtained from a study of the students' records and from the teacher's personal knowledge about the students.

Finally, 13 instructional processes available to teachers to help children in difficulty were described (for example, small-class instruction, flexible scheduling, extra homework) and it was determined whether the school was using these procedures for each student.

The intent was to use the data collected about students as a basis for developing an "At Risk Scale," which could be used to indicate the degree to which students were at risk. It was recognized at the outset that development of such a scale would have to be a preliminary effort; nevertheless, information about each student on each of the 45 factors was seen as useful in the development of such a scale.

To develop the "At Risk Scale," the research coordinating committee conceptualized a general definition of what it meant for a student to be "at risk." Following that, an eight-phase developmental effort was initiated.

First, general discussion produced agreement among the committee members that a student was at risk if that student was likely to fail in school or fail in life. In other words, if a student received failing grades in a course in school, was retained in a grade, or was likely to drop out of school, that student was thought to be at risk. Likewise, if a student used drugs, was sexually abused, lived in a home in which alcohol or drugs were used excessively, or had contemplated or attempted suicide, that student was assumed to be at risk. "Likely to fail in school or fail in life" was assumed to be a useful but general definition of what it means for a child to be "at risk."

Second, a careful review of the literature was undertaken to verify this general definition and to identify specific conditions that contributed to being at risk. More than 100 studies were examined.

Third, factors that contribute directly to at-riskness were identified from the research and specified in operational terms. Forty-five factors were identified and specified.

Fourth, a 45-item questionnaire predicated on the factors contributing to at-riskness was developed to verify the factors and to determine each factor's relative importance in the overall scale.

Fifth, 97 experienced educators responded to the questionnaire offering their judgment about the relative importance of each factor as contributing to at-riskness.

Sixth, following the determination of the relative importance of each factor by experienced educators, a weight was assigned to each factor in direct relationship to the value accorded that factor. Responses were summed for each item, and items then were listed in rank order according to the importance attributed to each item by those who had responded to the questionnaire. Each item was given the following weights:

- The top 9 items were given a weight of 5
- The next 9 items were given a weight of 4
- The next 9 items were given a weight of 3
- The next 9 items were given a weight of 2
- The next 7 items were given a weight of 1
- The next 2 items were given a weight of 0

Seventh, members of the chapter research team met with teachers or guidance counselors who knew the students well (and who had access to the students' records) and completed the "At Risk Scale" on each student selected for study (approximately 100 students in each school). The research team recorded the teacher's observations about each child on an "answer sheet" according to a student ID number for data analysis. If the teachers did not know the circumstances pertaining to a particular student, that item was left blank on the answer sheet.

Eighth, each answer sheet was scanned optically and the responses recorded on magnetic tape. Then an "At Risk Scale" score was determined for each student, according to the rationale and weighting described above. The number of "no response" items also was indicated, showing specific areas for which there was no information about a particular student.

The "At Risk Scale" score computed for each student, based on a careful study of the records of each student by teachers and others in each school, was acknowledged at the outset to be crude. Nevertheless, the research coordinating committee proceeded on the assumption that the basis for the "At Risk Scale" score (that is, factors identified by research, weighting by experienced educators, and logic of differentiated weighting) was a reasonable way to begin. But the committee also recognized that the score was neither final nor valid, and probably not reliable. It represented an initial effort to differentiate students on the basis of factual information; but extensive research will be required to substantiate the logic and assumptions used or, more likely, to modify the basic rationale.

A "School Effort" score was computed for each student on the basis of how many instructional strategies (of the 13 listed) were used with each student. Also, the relationship of school effort to at-riskness was determined.

Job 9, Do a Case Study: Each chapter also did a case study of one child. The tasks involved for the job required chapters to prepare a cumulative folder on the student, with names, addresses, and other identifying information removed, and to prepare two videotapes: one about the student and that youngster's home situation, and another about the school's effort to help that student. (Only 19 chapters produced the videotapes.) Finally, each chapter also prepared a two-part narrative about the student. Part one focused on the student and part two focused on the school's effort to help the student.

Job 10, Do at Least One Optional Project: In addition to the jobs outlined above, each participating chapter also did at least one optional project. Various alternatives were described in the *Manual of Instructions*, but any project that the chapter wanted to accomplish was allowed. The assumption was that a project of interest to the local chapter would be initiated and completed.

Job 11, Further Analyses of Data: For those chapters that were interested, the aggregated data were made available for further analyses. That is, if a chapter wanted to have access to the data pertaining to all of the principals, all of the teachers, or all of the students, the chapter submitted a proposal requesting access to the total data set. If the proposal was deemed acceptable, and if the chapter agreed to certain restrictions regarding use of the data (for example, not to reveal the name of any community, any person, or any chapter), the total data set was made available to the chapter for further analysis.

The intention in this part of the study was to encourage chapters whose members had special areas of expertise or special interests in the data to do further research. By making total data sets available, intensive analyses of various kinds were anticipated.

Job 12, Discuss the Data at District-Level Meetings: After the data had been collected and analyzed, representatives of participating chapters met in small-group meetings to discuss local and national data. Each chapter was provided with a printout of the student and teacher data collected at the local level, plus a computer disk with those same data that might be used for further analyses. In addition, summaries of the aggregated data from all chapters for all students, all teachers, and all principals were made available for discussion purposes.

The intent at these meetings was to try to answer the question: "What do these data mean?" By making all of the data available to the participating chapters, and by providing instruction at the meetings about how to analyze the data on a personal computer, it was hoped that local chapters would be capable of and interested in doing intensive analyses of their local data in comparison to the national data. Those analyses are now being worked on by the 87 chapters involved.

Finally, some suggestions about writing for professional publication were provided at the district-level meetings.

Job 13, Disseminate Research Results: Chapters participating in the project were encouraged to share the results of the research in any way that seemed appropriate for their communities: profession-

16

al publications, local chapter meetings, community organization meetings, or local media. It was assumed that dissemination of the results was important, and each participant was instructed and encouraged to share the results through whatever outlets seemed appropriate.

Chapter Three
From Data Collection to Discussion

Reasonably complete sets of data were collected by 87 chapters between 10 October and 15 December 1988. Materials were mailed to Phi Delta Kappa Headquarters before the end of December. Of the 100 chapters selected to participate in the project, 13 failed to complete the data collection activities in time for their data to be included in the final analysis.

Materials received at Phi Delta Kappa were separated according to the nature of the data (for example, principal interviews, teacher surveys), and a record was made of items received and items missing from each participating chapter.

Descriptions of how the schools were selected and narrative descriptions of the three schools were collected together and stored at Headquarters for use by the research coordinating committee in preparing the final report.

Principal interviews were coded and entered by hand into a word-processing program in 80-column, non-document mode format for later statistical analysis.

The Holding Power Statistic information was entered into a spreadsheet program for later statistical analysis.

"Teacher Survey" and "Information About Students" forms were collected and taken to the Indianapolis Public Schools Computer Division for optical scanning in early January 1989. All forms were scanned, and computer tapes were readied for statistical analysis by mid-January.

Preparing Materials for Participating Chapters

The computer tapes were mailed to the Bureau of Educational Research at the University of Virginia for analysis during the third week of January. At the university, six things were done: each tape was reviewed for errors, special tapes were prepared, printouts were prepared, computer disks were prepared, computer programs were prepared, and printed materials were prepared to help participating chapters use the disks and printouts that had been generated. Each of these six operations is described below.

The optical scan used to produce computer tapes was carried out following specifications developed by the research coordinating committee member who was a specialist in computer operations. After the tapes were received at the University of Virginia, the records on each tape (one for teacher data and one for student data) were examined for errors, line by line, and corrections made.

Once the integrity of the data had been determined, four sets of data files were prepared. One set of files aggregated the data for all teachers; one set of files aggregated the data for all students. Separate files were developed for the teacher data and the student data for each participating chapter.

Following that, more than 200 computer runs were accomplished with the Statistical Package for Social Sciences (SPSS) on a mainframe computer. One set of runs produced an analysis of teachers' responses to the "Teacher Survey," chapter by chapter. A second set of runs produced analyses of the aggregated data from teachers. A third set of runs produced analyses of the information collected about students on the "Information About Students" form, chapter by chapter. A fourth set produced analyses of the aggregated data about students. Each computer run resulted in a printout or series of printouts. All printouts were mailed to Phi Delta Kappa Headquarters in early February 1989.

Next, disks were prepared that could be used for statistical analysis at the local level on microcomputers. In all, 87 disks were prepared. A disk included all of the data collected about students and about teachers for a particular chapter.

Twelve computer programs were developed at the University of Virginia for participating chapters to use in analyzing their data at the local level. Six of the programs were designed to be modified and used on a mainframe computer; six were designed to be used on a microcomputer. Some of the programs did crosstabs analyses, others did frequency analyses. One program computed the "At Risk Scale" score for individual students, and another computed the "School Effort" score for each student. All of these computer programs were put on the disks that had been prepared for each chapter.

By February 15, printed materials were developed that enabled chapter participants to use the special computer programs and disks to accomplish whatever analyses they thought would be most useful and most appropriate in their situation. Instructions spelled out which data were recorded in which column, how many lines an individual record occupied, file names, value labels, variable labels, how to verify data, and the like.

Copies of sample programs designed to help participants do various statistical analyses were developed so participants could use their data and the SPSS/PC+ program on their own microcomputer.

Sixteen chapters submitted proposals requesting access to data from all of the chapters for further analysis. Those proposals were reviewed by a committee at Phi Delta Kappa Headquarters. Those chapters whose proposals were accepted received special magnetic tapes and computer disks in late February 1989. Reports were due in August 1989.

Discussing the Data

All of the printed materials and computer disks were assembled and shipped so they could be used by chapter participants in small-group meetings held at seven sites around the country. The dates and sites for these district-level meetings were:

Orlando, Florida (March 10 to 12)
San Francisco (March 24 to 26)
Chicago (March 31 to April 2)
Washington, D.C. (April 7 to 9)
Seattle (April 14 to 16)
Dallas (April 21 to 23)
Omaha (April 28 to 30)

Each of the district-level meetings included 10 to 20 persons from participating chapters and two or three people from the research coordinating committee. The study director was present at all meetings.

Although these district-level meetings were similar in many respects, each was also unique. The topics addressed and activities engaged in during the three-day meetings were: sharing experiences among participants, distribution of materials, explanation of the "At Risk Scale" score, examination of data in terms of research questions, review of how data were stored on the disk, instructions and practice in analyzing data on a microcomputer, asking the right questions, and writing for professional publication. Each of these topics or activities is described below.

Each meeting started with participants introducing themselves and sharing something about the chapter research committee structure they established, the processes they used, and successes and problems they encountered during the course of conducting the study.

Next, the following sets of materials were distributed to each person:

- Manual (computer programs)
- Printout of local student data
- Printout of local teacher data
- Printout of local "At Risk Scale" scores
- Printout of "School Effort" scores
- Summary of all student data
- Summary of all teacher data
- Summary of all principal data
- Summary of Holding Power Statistic data
- Disk with local data and computer programs
- Articles about writing for publication

The "At Risk Scale" score was explained. It will be recalled that the Phi Delta Kappa Study of Students at Risk began by posing four questions: Who is at risk? What are they like? What are the schools doing to help these students? How effective are those efforts? In the materials distributed to each participant, "At Risk Scale" scores were included for each student for whom data had been collected in the three schools in which the participant's chapter collected data.

The rationale behind the "At Risk Scale" score and the process by which the score was computed were explained earlier. As pointed out, the research coordinating committee that developed the scale thought the items were defensible, but they were uncomfortable with doing a simple summation of items. Therefore, the committee developed the weighted score scale. However, even though the rationale was explicit and reasonable, several factors made any interpretation of the scores questionable.

First, students for whom information was limited would receive a lower score simply because an item could not be tallied unless information about the student was available. In practical terms, that meant that scores of students about whom teachers had little information would tend to be lower. Second, several of the items were more applicable to secondary students than to elementary students (for example, pregnancy and use of alcohol). Thus scores for elementary students would typically be lower than scores for secondary students. Finally, the range of scores produced during the first analysis was so great (0 to 120) but the mean so low (7 for elementary students and 9 for senior high school students) that interpreting the data required great caution.

Much time was devoted to helping participants understand the problems associated with interpreting the "At Risk Scale" scores. Participants were encouraged to develop their own scores by working with the schools involved and were advised to use great care in sharing the scores with principals and teachers, making sure they understood the complexities and nuances in interpreting the scores.

Another activity for participants involved studying printouts — local data and total data — and to answer the questions, "Who is at risk?" and "What are they like?" The intent was to help participants get a "feel" for the data — from their own community and from the total sample — and to explore the data in ways that would be useful and interesting.

On the second day, participants spent most of the time learning to use SPSS/PC + on a microcomputer and asking important questions about the research data. They had an opportunity to run a simple program, get into their own data file, get comfortable with SPSS/PC + on a microcomputer, and develop a sense of what might be possible once they got back home. In addition, they were encouraged to think about which questions ought to be examined in depth, which were not worth pursuing, and ways of using the available database to answer the important questions.

Finally, a two-hour session on writing for professional publication explored the ins and outs of publishing: how to prepare a manuscript, where to send it, what to expect from an editor, how to increase the probability of getting a manuscript accepted, and the like.

Chapter Four
Overview of the Results

Data on 22,018 students were collected by participating chapters in 87 communities using the definitions and procedures described in Chapter Three. The students were fairly evenly divided among the three grade levels involved: 6,173 fourth-graders, 7,762 seventh-graders, 7,417 tenth-graders, and 666 others. In all, 70% were white, 16% black, 7% Hispanic, 2% native American, and 3% Asian. Almost 51% were male; 49% were female.

In addition, the records of all first-time ninth-graders who enrolled in each of 95 high schools in the fall of 1984 (N = 27,250) were studied over time to determine the Holding Power Statistic for each school.

Data also were collected from 276 principals through a structured interview: 94 elementary principals, 86 middle or junior high principals, and 96 senior high school principals were involved. Within the group, 86% were white and 10% black; 77% were male and 23% female. The interview inclued 159 questions.

All of the teachers in each of the 276 schools were asked to respond to a 116-item survey instrument about at-risk students and school practices. A total of 9,652 teachers completed the surveys: 22% were elementary teachers, 30% were middle or junior high teachers, and 48% were senior high school teachers. Of those interviewed, 85% were white, 6% black, 2% Hispanic, and 2% Asian. Sixty-five percent were female; 35% were male.

Data were analyzed two ways. First, they were aggregated for all 276 schools, and descriptive analyses were accomplished. This chapter is based on those analyses of aggregated data.

Second, data were analyzed separately by site (that is, by chapter) and by school. Separate analyses were conducted by each chapter to provide information that would be useful and important to those in the local community. Separate analyses also were conducted by the research coordinating committee to test the idea of simultaneous replication as a research methodology.

Findings that Pertain to Students

Recall the instructions for researchers to select "typical" students:

> . . . *do not select students who are in special groups for inclusion in this study.* Do not select students who have been assigned full-time to classrooms for the mentally retarded, for example. Do not select students who are assigned full-time to programs in alternative schools. Select "typical" students in the school.

And when those who knew the student best and who had immediate access to the records did not know or did not have the information requested, the instructions were explicit:

> *If the information is not available* − in the student's folder, in the school's records, or in the teacher's experience, *leave that space unmarked on the answer blank.*

It is important to keep these considerations in mind. Some of the data reported below do not "square" with reports in the general media. The discrepancies may be a function of the fact that, although the sample was large, it was not selected according to conventional statistical criteria to ensure representativeness (after all, chapters volunteered). More important, the discrepancy may be explained by the fact that teachers and others who knew the students best often did not have pertinent information about risk factors.

It was assumed that any student characterized as evidencing six or more of the 45 factors used to define at-riskness in this study was seriously at risk. Using that crude definition, one-fourth to one-third of the 22,018 students whose records were examined were identified as seriously at risk. In other words, if a student had six strikes against him or her, that student was at risk.

Note that these data are conservative. Any student for whom there was no information on certain factors was not judged to be at risk on those factors, even though additional information might have indicated that the student actually was at risk. In other words, the information reported here was always biased in a low direction, never in a high direction. Future reports will outline the extent of at-riskness in terms of weighted "At Risk Scale" scores and subscores.

About 55% of the 22,018 students whose records were studied lived in a home with the traditional mother/father relationship; 35% lived in a different kind of home setting (for example, real mother/step-father, mother only, or foster home), and 10% of the home situations were not known.

One out of seven students had been retained in grade at least once. One out of seven failed at least one course in the year before the study. One out of six was at least one year older than the other students in that student's grade in school.

One out of 15 students missed 21 or more days of school in the year before the study. One out of 18 was suspended from school at least once in the year before the study. Three out of 10 had attended three or more schools during the past five years. Five out of 100 lived in homes in which English was not the first language. Four out of 10 did not participate in extracurricular activities. One out of eight had a negative sense of self-esteem.

Three out of 100 students used drugs in the year before the study; at the high school level the ratio was nine out of a 100. Three out of 100 students lived with family members who used drugs in the year before the study; at the high school level the ratio was seven out of 100. One out of 100 students sold drugs in the year before the study; the ratio was two out of 100 at the high school level. One out of 100 students had attempted suicide; three out of 100 at the high school level. Two out of 100 students had been physically or sexually abused; three out of 100 at the high school level. Five out of 100 students used alcohol in the year before the study; 15 out of 100 at the high school level. One out of 100 students was involved in a pregnancy in the year before the study; two out of 100 at the high school level.

Male students are more at risk than females. Blacks, Hispanics, and native Americans are more at risk than whites or Asians.

Not reflected in the above data are the instances in which teachers and others who knew the students best reported "do not know" in response to the questions asked. For example, the proportion of cases in which teachers responded "do not know" about drug use by students was 22%; family members using drugs, 32%; students selling drugs, 23%; student suicide attempts, 29%; physical or sexual abuse,

26%; students using alcohol, 24%; pregnancies among students, 22%.

In 50% of the cases, teachers did not know the father's level of education; in 25% of the cases, they did not know the father's occupation. Teachers did not know the mother's level of education in 45% of the cases; they did not know the mother's occupation in 19% of the cases. In 35% of the cases, they did not know whether the student's parents had had a major change in health status during the past year. In 27% of the cases, they did not know whether a student's parent had died. In 37% of the cases, they did not know whether a parent had lost his or her job. In 28% of the cases, they did not know if a divorce or separation had occurred. In 32% of the cases, teachers did not know if a sibling had dropped out of school. In 17% of the cases, teachers did not know the student well enough to estimate that student's sense of self-esteem.

Schools did more things (that is, employed more "School Effort" techniques) for students who had higher "At Risk Scale" scores than for students who had lower scores. However, more than one-third of the most severely at-risk students received less than two of the 13 instructional strategies that constituted the "School Effort" score. The mean for all students was three.

The Holding Power Statistic was computed for 95 high schools by tracing the records of all students who entered high school as first-time ninth-graders in the fall of 1984. Holding power varied greatly among schools, with a mean Holding Power Statistic of 81%. Holding power was defined as the capacity of the school to hold students from ninth grade through graduation, while accounting for students who did not complete high school.

Findings that Pertain to Teachers

When teachers were asked who was responsible for various areas of learning, they responded in traditional ways. Teachers accepted responsibility for helping students in the areas of reading, writing, mathematics, and higher-order thinking skills, but thought that parents and students were responsible for students' daily attendance, listening, attitude toward school, completion of homework, general behavior in school, and attention in class.

Asked whether they thought it was possible for teachers to help students cope with various out-of-school problems, more than 60% of the teachers responded negatively regarding such problems as family discord, family instability, crime, and alcohol abuse; 45% reported that they could not help students cope with substance abuse. In more than 90% of the cases, teachers thought that parents or students rather than teachers should be most responsible for helping students cope with those problems. Teachers' efforts to help students who were most at risk were restricted to the academic realm.

Four out of 10 teachers reported that they regularly retained students in grade, and almost half (48%) maintained that retention was effective.

Findings that Pertain to Principals

In terms of changes that had taken place in schools in recent years and that affected all students, including those at risk, three out of four principals reported that their schools had increased graduation requirements and adopted mandatory testing of students. Seven out of 10 principals reported that they regularly retained students in grade, though only one out of four thought retention was effective. Six out of 10 reported that their schools restricted participation in sports for low achievers.

Chapter Five
Issues that Emerged

This research study grew out of educational issues likely to be considered crucial by 1990. During the course of the research, other issues emerged. Seven of those emerging issues are examined in this chapter. The discussion goes beyond the data generated in this study in order to focus attention on research that could and should be done.

Each issue is described in terms of how it evolved and took shape in this project, but most are rooted in practice and beliefs that extend beyond the scope of this project. Although the issues are set forth here as discrete realities, all are interrelated in inextricable ways. Like most important problems, they do not lend themselves to simple solutions.

Two issues — research and retention — serve as themes or strands to tie all of the issues together. The seven issues that became apparent during the conduct of this study are:

1. Discrepancies regarding practice and belief.
2. Lack of information about students.
3. Retaining students in grade.
4. Measuring at-riskness.
5. Reality of individual differences.
6. Costs and benefits.
7. Place of research in a profession.

Discrepancies Regarding Practice and Belief

Various data suggest that the professionals surveyed in this project expressed discrepancies between their practices and beliefs that related to working with at-risk students. For example, 99% of the principals reported that they regularly notified parents when they worked with students who were at risk; 68% said notifying parents was effective. And 99% said they regularly conferred with parents of students who were at risk; 74% thought such conferences were effective. Likewise, 82% maintained that they regularly referred at-risk students to a psychologist; 61% reported that the practice was effective. Almost three-fourths (71%) said they regularly retained students in grade, but only one-fourth (26%) thought retention was effective. And 73% assigned at-risk students to low-ability groups, but only 44% thought such practice was effective.

Among teachers, 95% reported that they regularly notified parents of at-risk students; 79% said notification was effective. Asked whether they regularly conferred with parents of at-risk sudents, 94% of the teachers reported that they did; 81% stated that such conferences were effective.

Less than half of the students who were most seriously at risk in grades seven and 10 received any of the 13 "School Effort" strategies other than extra parental involvement and more emphasis on basic skills.

Though teachers and administrators were generally positive about using various techniques to help at-risk students, they seemed to lack confidence that such techniques were effective. In several areas, teachers reported that certain teaching techniques frequently were effective, although they did not use such techniques regularly. For example, 91% said individualizing instruction was effective; 79% said they did it regularly. And although 81% of the teachers stated that peer tutoring was effective, only 63% reported that they used peer tutoring regularly. Yet these were techniques over which teachers had complete control.

In several areas, discrepancies between the use and effectiveness data suggest that teachers thought someone else should help them with the problem. For example, 79% of the teachers reported that vocational courses would be effective for at-risk students; 50% said such courses were available. Before-school programs would be effective, said 63% of the teachers; 42% reported that they used such programs. More than two-thirds of the teachers (69%) said that alternative school opportunities would be effective for at-risk students; 37% of the teachers provided such opportunities. Teacher aides would be effective, said 77% of the teachers; 48% reported that they used such programs. And 70% thought that referring an at-risk student to a social worker was effective, but only 54% said that they regularly made such referrals. Special teachers were effective, said 85% of the teachers; but only 67% of the teachers regularly used such special teachers. Special textbooks were effective with at-risk students, said 71% of the teachers; but only 48% reported that they regularly used such textbooks. The same is true for flexible scheduling; 69% of the teachers reported that such scheduling was effective, but only 48% of the teachers said they used it.

Some of these discrepancies may be attributed to the fact that professionals do not know how to use such techniques, or they are unable to persuade others to help them use them. Other discrepancies may be a function of idealism; that is, teachers may want to use more effective techniques, but in practice they don't. This is an area that needs further study.

Lack of Information About Students

One of the major findings of this study was that certain kinds of information were generally not available to teachers and others in the schools.

There probably were several reasons that professionals in schools were unable to provide the information requested in this study: concerns about confidentiality, poor record-keeping practices, philosophical differences about what information is important for teachers to have, administrative convenience, and practical considerations of this type of research.

Some of the chapter data collectors reported difficulty gaining access to information about students that was perceived as confidential, even though the names of students were never revealed to the data collectors. Probably more important was that many schools did not maintain student records in ways that gave teachers or others in the building ready access to them. For example, some districts did not transmit information about students from one school to another or from one level to another. The only information available was what the professionals in a particular building had put in a student folder themselves. Under such circumstances, it was not surprising that teachers and counselors knew very little about incoming students who were new seventh-graders in a junior high school, for instance. Selden (1988) outlined this same problem in terms of state-level demands on schools for student data. The problem appears to be exacerbated by the fact that schools have no agreed-on way to collect and use data about students.

When confronted with the fact that little personal information on students was available, some teachers and counselors said that such information could bias the teacher. Their rationale went something like this: teachers who have information, for example, about a child's home background, may label or stereotype that child. Knowing anything about a student's home situation might bias a teacher's perspective. Others disagreed with that position, arguing that teachers could not help a student about whom they knew very little. Those teachers were convinced that they needed to know if a child came from a broken home or if a parent was an alcoholic or unemployed. Some of the chapter data collectors thought it was inappropriate to ask teachers to provide information about children that was not readily available. This is understandable; but the fact remains that without such information, a school is limited in what it can do to to help young people who are at risk.

Another factor contributing to the lack of student information is the attitude among some educators that they can deal with the problems of at-risk students by collecting and analyzing the most readily available data collected by the schools: grades, attendance figures, and achievement test scores. They do this because such data is convenient, even though they know that factors such as a parent's loss of job or a student's use of alcohol or drugs may affect the student's learning and behavior dramatically. To ignore data about out-of-school factors because they are not readily available or because they raise issues regarding confidentiality puts professionals in the position of dealing with symptoms rather than causes.

If nonacademic factors contribute to at-riskness (and they do), teachers and counselors who do not have access to such information or do not take the time to seek it will never know some of the most important factors affecting student learning. One is reminded of the story of the drunk who was looking under the lamp post for his lost key. When asked, "Is that where you lost the key?" he answered, "No, but the light is better here."

There is no agreement within the profession regarding what kinds of student data are necessary for teachers to be effective. There is no standardized case history or cumulative record form that professionals generally agree is important to maintain. Cost, administrative convenience, and school philosophy affect the the way a school maintains records on each student. These factors influence whether that record is updated periodically, whether it is used regularly by staff, and what disposition is made of the record when the student moves to another school or leaves the district.

A final consideration is the different orientation researchers and teachers have about student data. Schools have been criticized in recent years for asking students "personal" questions, and "human subjects clearance" has become a major issue confronting researchers who work in schools. As a result of such concerns, researchers studying young people's behavior must ensure anonymity for students' responses to questionnaires (after clearance).

Two questions then arise. Are the responses valid? That is, were the students honest in their answers? Can we have confidence in what they reported on the questionnaire regarding their behavior about smoking, alcohol, sex, drugs, or suicide attempts? But teachers want to know the answer to a second question: Who are the students who indicated that they smoked or drank or engaged in sex or whatever? Who are those young people, so we can help them?

For example, if 34% of the students in middle schools reported anonymously on questionnaires that they regularly used drugs, the question teachers and administrators want answered is: Which students? Who is involved? Data about students in general are not particularly helpful. Professionals want to help, but they do not know which students are involved. Even so, the public demands that "schools must do something" to help such students.

Some argue that teachers do know who the abused and the abusers are. Maybe. Maybe not. The data in this study were clear: if teachers knew who those students were, they did not always identify them to the researchers, even by ID number. This presents a quandary. The general public is regularly informed (on the basis of anonymous responses to questionnaires) that such and such a proportion of youth are "regular drinkers" or "drug users" or "engaged in sexual activity" or "come from broken homes." But teachers and administrators in schools often think they are denied the right to query students directly on such matters.

Thus the issue was drawn. Schools in this study often lacked information about students that might help teachers and others deal with at-riskness in helpful ways. It is an old issue, of course; but it emerged full-blown in this project. This issue warrants further study.

Retaining Students in Grade

Retaining students in grade was the only school-imposed factor of the 45 used in this study that previous research indicated contributed to at-riskness. Retention in grade is something a school does to a student and is not a decision based on where the student lived, what the parents did or did not do, or how the student felt about himself or herself. Keep in mind that of the 22,018 students whose records were examined in this study, 14% had been retained in grade at least one time.

There have been many studies of retention. Some have examined how parents, teachers, or administrators felt about retaining in grade. Other studies analyzed school board policies or district practices. The most telling studies looked at the impact of retention on students' achievement, persistence, self-concept, dropout rates, and graduation rates. This latter kind of research consistently concludes that retaining students in grade is generally harmful: the probability of dropping out of school is increased, and the likelihood of raising achievement levels is decreased (Grissom and Shepard 1988). There are exceptions to this general rule, of course; but they are exceptions. Among most knowledgeable researchers, the effect of retention in grade is not an issue (Holmes 1988). It is a decided fact.

But more than 40% of the teachers and more than 70% of the principals in this project reported that they regularly retained students in grade. Further, 48% of the teachers and 26% of the principals responded that retention was effective in dealing with at-risk students. How can this discrepancy between research and practice be explained? Several factors may be involved: legal mandates, skepticism about research, effect of personal experience, and the role of punishment in education. Each of these factors is discussed below.

Traditionally, teachers and administrators have turned to the law and personal experience rather than research as a basis for justifying their practices. If the law mandates a certain practice in schools, educators comply with the law, even if they know that the mandate is harmful rather than helpful. Some legislatures have required schools to retain in grade children who do not achieve at a specified level of achievement. Despite what the research says, educators obey the law.

Further, teachers and administrators have confidence in their own personal and professional experience as a basis for generalizing about professional practice; they do not always have confidence in research findings. Direct experience is more immediate and to them more valid as a basis for making decisions than the indirect experience of research. And people in education often say about research: "That does not apply to me. Our school is different. My situation is unique."

The tendency to rely on legal mandates or personal experience rather than research as a basis for generalizing about professional practice is troubling. Nevertheless, teachers' motives are well intentioned. They want to help students. They think that retaining students who lack certain skills is preferable to putting them in a situation at the next level where they will face more frustration and more failure.

Research on school retention is clear: if students who are retained are provided new experiences and special help, such students may benefit from being retained in grade. However, most schools do not do anything different for students who are retained; and most students who are retained in grade do not benefit. The child "repeats" the grade and does the same things that he or she did the year before. Research that would be helpful might focus on interventions that proved effective when students were retained. What do schools do differently that is helpful to youngsters who are held back? How can educators assure themselves, their students, and those students' parents that retention will not mean repetition of that which was unsuccessful before?

Among children who might have been retained under other circumstances but were promoted, research shows that they did better than children who were retained. It may be that promoted children did better simply because they encountered new experiences in the next grade; they did not "repeat" the same experience or go through the same materials again. In other words, promotion guarantees new experiences. Do the new experiences outweigh the supposed benefits of being held back to master the concepts and skills assigned to various grade levels by schools? Why do promoted students generally do better than those who were retained? These questions deserve further study.

Retaining a child in grade may be viewed by some as punishment for not learning. "If he does not learn, I'll show him. I'll hold him back a year." Punishment has always been one dimension of most educators' belief systems. Punishing children who violate social norms or school rules about general behavior is appropriate. But is it appropriate to punish children who do not learn to read, do not learn their multiplication tables, or do not learn their parts of speech? What if they cannot learn? And do teachers distinguish between a child who refuses to learn from one who cannot learn? What if a teacher is convinced that a student tried hard all year but must be retained because a building administrator or district policy or state law stipulates that low achievers must be retained in grade? This problem deserves careful study.

The question for educators is: Whose welfare is most important? Should schools serve the welfare of the people outside the school (that is, parents, taxpayers, employers) or the people inside the school (students)? How can students' welfare be best served?

Those who develop and implement public policy in education have not always sorted through such questions, nor have educators been particularly effective in helping policy makers focus on the central issues in ways that optimize what happens to young people in schools. Who is the primary client? Who is the school really supposed to help? Will the proposed policies be helpful or harmful to children in school? Should parents have any say in whether their child is promoted or retained? What information would be most appropriate for parents in those circumstances? Can schools involve parents in such decisions without manipulating the outcome? These questions warrant further study.

Measuring At-Riskness

The research reported here began with a review of the research on factors that contribute to at-riskness. The intention from the outset was to develop an instrument or scale to measure at-riskness that would be both valid and practical for educators to use. In attempting to develop an index of at-riskness, two models were considered, the medical model and the psychiatric model.

The medical model can be illustrated by describing the approach to dealing with coronary heart disease. Typically, a patient is assessed to be at risk of heart attack on the basis of the following factors: family history, cholesterol levels, smoking, hypertension, obesity, and level of exercise. The probability of each factor is assessed, but the interactive effects of several factors are also determined.

Psychiatrists deal with the complexities of human behavior by distinguishing between two things: predisposing factors (those that develop over a long period of time, usually more than two years), and short-term life events, which are usually of short duration (six months or less). Examples of the long-term predisposing factors would include such things as marital discord in a home over a period of years or long-term unemployment. Short-term life events such as the loss of a loved one, divorce, or an unplanned pregnancy illustrate the second category. Psychiatrists presume that short-term life events may affect persons who have predisposing factors and accelerate the deterioration of an individual's mental health.

Using such models as a way of thinking about at-riskness, the researchers in this project began by agreeing on 45 factors that previous research indicated contributed to students being at risk. It was not assumed that these factors caused at-riskness but rather that there might be an associative relationship between one or more of the factors and at-risk behavior. If one of the factors was present in a student's life, that factor was assumed to be a symptom of at-riskness that might make the individual more vulnerable to other factors present in the environment.

Second, it was assumed that different students would cope with and respond to particular aspects of their environment in different ways. Some students handle the death of a parent reasonably well; others collapse under the burden of such a loss. Some students are spurred on to try harder by receiving low grades in school; others are overwhelmed and give up.

Information regarding each of the 45 factors was collected on each of the 22,018 students whose school records were examined in this study. That information was looked at in terms of three questions: Was the information available? Was the student affected by the at-risk factors that had been operationally defined on the basis of previous research? And what was the degree of at-riskness present in the student's life as represented by the the student's "At Risk Scale" score?

Patterns were presumed to be more important than individual instances, as far as the 45 factors were involved. That is, a pregnant girl who was taking drugs and who had attempted suicide was more at risk than a student who moved last year and failed one test in school. But the interaction of a particular student with a particular set of circumstances was always thought to be the reality that had to be assessed, difficult as that might prove to be.

What has been reported in this monograph represents the "first cut" of the data that were collected about students at risk. Future studies will validate the factors, determine the relationships or patterns that exist among factors, and determine the relationships between those patterns and actual evidence of at-risk behavior as manifested by the subsequent behavior of students whose records were studied. In other words, subsequent analyses of the data (and additional data collected over time on some of the students) may result in the development of a scale to measure at-riskness. Such a scale is not now available, except in preliminary form. Longitudinal studies, validation studies, and reliability studies may ultimately prove the "At Risk Scale" useful. In its present form, it is strictly an experimental instrument in need of refinement.

The Reality of Individual Differences

Students are different, and comprehending and coping with individual differences emerged as an issue deserving further study.

In this study, 70% of the students were white, 16% black, 7% Hispanic, 2% native American, and 3% Asian. In terms of family grouping, 55% of the students lived with their real mother and real father, 10% with their real mother and stepfather, 2% with their real father and stepmother, 16% with the real mother only, 2% with the real father only, 3% in an extended family situation, 1% in a foster home or institution, and 10% were not known. These data confirm what other studies have shown: America is changing demographically, and students cannot be characterized in monolithic ways (Hodgkinson 1985; Pallas, Natriello, and McDill 1989).

In terms of parents' education, 32% of the mothers and 27% of the fathers had a high school education or less; but in almost half of the cases, the parents' educational background was not known. Approximately 30% of the fathers and 20% of the mothers worked as professionals, managers, or technicians; and 45% of the fathers and 60% of the mothers worked as skilled or unskilled laborers (or were unemployed). But in more than a fifth of the cases, the parents' occupations were not known.

Students differed in terms of their scores on standardized achievement tests, intelligence tests, grades, participation in extracurricular activities, sense of self-esteem, changes of residence, number of schools attended, health status, parents' health status, and in other ways. But much information in these areas was not available from the school.

More blacks (40%), Hispanics (38%), and native Americans (42%) were at risk than white (20%) or Asian (20%) children. More males (29%) were at risk than females (21%). Older students (32%) were more at risk than younger students (21%), and students in certain schools and certain communities were more at risk than students in other schools and communities.

The extent to which students are or are not at risk is reflected in data such as these, but there was no such thing as a "typical" student. And school programs that presume there is "one best way" of working with at-risk students are not likely to be effective. Since students are different, there can never be "one best way" that will be appropriate and effective for all students.

The data in this study suggest that the reality of individual differences was not always fully comprehended by the teachers and others who provided information about individual students in this study. The "do not know" response was often recorded on the questionnaire.

America is committed to achieving and maintaining a socially integrated but heterogeneous society. Diversity is valued. Differences are important. The data in this study raised questions about what teachers knew about how their students differed, what those differences meant, and how the teachers coped with differences in their classrooms. Questions for further study arise.

How do teachers learn the complexities and nuances of individual differences? Have they learned which differences make a difference in learning and which do not? Have they acquired the professional skills and procedures for ascertaining differences among their students? How do teachers' beliefs about individual differences influence what those teachers do in classrooms? These questions are worthy of further study.

Costs and Benefits

Teachers and administrators often use a cost-and-benefit rationale when they talk about practices in education. The phrase, "costs and benefits," implies an equation, a balance. People expect to pay for certain gains. What does research show?

Returning to the issue of retention in grade, research makes it clear that children who are retained in grade are much more likely to drop out of school than children who are not retained (Shepard and Smith 1988; Unstattd and Thornton 1960; Otto and Estes 1960; Anderson and Ritscher 1969). Furthermore, the achievement of children who are retained in grade is almost always lower than the achievement of similar children who were promoted (Holmes and Matthews 1984). Finally, the impact of retention on self-concept and self-esteem is almost always negative. Special attention from parents or teachers or both may produce results different from those described in the research, but such variation is always the exception rather than the rule. Public policy and professional practice should be based on rules, not exceptions. And the rule is: Children who are retained in grade are generally harmed by the experience. It costs a lot for individuals and for society to have a student repeat a grade.

And the benefits? If the pattern of previous research on grade retention is correct, and it is difficult to refute the hundreds of studies and thoughtful analyses that have been done over the past 85 years, the benefits are generally nil. In other words, retaining students in grade seems to be all cost and no benefit — both to the nation and to the individuals.

Of the 22,018 students whose records were examined in this study, 14% had been retained in grade one or more years (in 8% of the cases, no information was available). Last year the average expenditure per pupil to educate students in the United States was $4,509 (NEA 1989). Using that figure as a base, it is apparent that taxpayers had to spend $14 million to reteach the students in this study who had been retained in grade.

Accepting the fact that the sampling in this study makes it difficult to generalize to the population as a whole, the data collected in this study still suggest that retaining students in grade is a major problem in schools and a costly problem for society. For example, if the data in this study are even reasonably correct, approximately 5.6 million students in the United States (14% of the total school population of 40 million students) have repeated a grade during the past 12 years. Thus it cost taxpayers about $25 billion to reteach students who were retained. That amounts to more than $2 billion per year over the 12-year span of school.

Generalizations such as this are dangerous, of course, given that the sample for this study is not truly representative of the nation. But there is no reason to believe the figures reported in this research project are too high; the data here actually understate the problem. Shepard and Smith, who reviewed the national data, maintain that the retention rate in the United States is much higher than the 14% over 12 years that is reported in this study; it is probably at least twice that high (Shepard and Smith 1988; Levin 1989).

Such estimates may not be completely accurate for reasons other than the non-representativeness of the sample. For example, retaining a student increases the probability that the student will drop out of school later, so society will not have to spend $4,509 per year for each student who drops out. However, young people who drop out of school are more likely to cost society in other ways – they sometimes require unemployment compensation, they typically pay lower taxes, they may force society to pay the costs of incarceration, and they often require social welfare services – thus actually increasing the total cost to society.

Likewise, costs to individuals for being retained are not included in the direct costs to society. What does the loss of pride, lower self-esteem, and lack of aspirations mean for those who are retained in grade? Are they more likely or less likely to become achievers and producers? Are they more likely or less likely to become responsible, independent human beings? Are they more likely or less likely to develop special skills and special abilities? Are they more likely or less likely to be contributors to society?

Is it defensible for educators to make decisions that force society to spend billions of dollars every year when they require children to repeat an experience that will probably not be helpful and may actually increase the likelihood that those children will become even more at risk? Existing research is clear: Retaining students in grade is costly for society and for the individual. Politically, it may be expedient to retain students. Educationally, it is indefensible, except under narrowly defined conditions. Accountability to the general public is an issue here.

Many questions arise. What are the true costs of retention to society and to the individual, in both dollars and human terms? Do teachers and administrators know what the true costs are? Do taxpayers and employers know what the true costs are? Do professionals and taxpayers think that such costs are appropriate and reasonable? Do they think the costs are worth the benefits that accrue? Do they accept the fact that they have to pay such costs through taxes? Such questions should be examined in detail. This whole problem area must be studied from the cost/benefit perspective.

Place of Research in a Profession

Most educators think of themselves as professionals; at least they aspire to professional status. What does it mean to be professional? What is the place of research in a profession?

The word "professional" implies two things: that people who are called "professionals" have had special training and possess special skills, and they get paid for using their training and skills. Physicians are referred to as professionals because they have had special training and possess special skills, but certain athletes are described as professionals because they get paid for doing what other people do for fun.

Sociologists have studied professionals as a subgroup of the workforce (Parsons 1939; Vollmer and Mills 1966; Cogan 1953). Research on the subject of professionalism suggests that those persons and those groups that are truly professional are characterized in six ways.

First, professionals provide service to others; they help other people. But the service provided is not a luxury; it is essential. If a person has a ruptured appendix, that person needs assistance and cannot resolve that problem alone.

Second, professionals have special skills that they employ in helping other people; and those skills can be taught and they can be learned. Nobody is born knowing how to counsel an alcoholic, perform a root canal, draw up a contract, or tie a suture. Professional schools teach people how to do those kinds of things.

Third, professionals base what they do on the best research information available. Physicians, for example, do not belong to the Christian Science Church simply because that church advocates methods of healing that are not empirically verifiable. Every truly professional group has a solid research base that guides practice.

Fourth, professionals make decisions that affect other people; and the people who are affected (clients) often do not know if the decisions are correct. For example, if a physician tells a patient he needs open-heart surgery, the patient does not know whether the physician is correct or incorrect. The patient can get a second opinion but never really knows whether the proposed procedure is appropriate or required. Although there is always a possibility of exploitation, clients must trust what professionals say and do.

Fifth, because the professional-client relationship is based on trust, and because the opportunity for exploitation is always there, those persons and groups that are truly professional operate under a set of ethical principles, which are designed to guarantee that professionals provide the highest quality service to those they help. In that sense, "professional," "ethical," and "effective" are synonymous terms.

Sixth, those who are truly professional use their professional organizations to guarantee that every member adheres to ethical principles. Practitioners who behave in ways that are not in the best interest of clients, or who violate ethical principles, or who conduct their practice based on dogma or personal whim rather than research are disciplined or denied the right to practice. Lawyers are disbarred. Physicians lose their license to practice.

Using these six characteristics of professionalism provides a way to think about education as a profession. For example, take the role of research in education. There have been many research studies in the area of individual differences over the years. What do teachers know about individual differences? Have preservice programs helped prospective teachers learn what research says about which differences make a difference in learning? Do school districts provide inservice programs to help teachers understand how learning styles affect the way students learn? Has the "child study" approach that served teachers so well in the past been abandoned? If so, why? These questions need to be examined through research.

The lack of a research orientation may explain why so many "do not know" responses were made by teachers to questions regarding students. The data in this study suggest that teachers who had access to students' records were generally able to provide information about students' academic backgrounds but were less able to provide information about students' home backgrounds. Does this suggest that the relationship between school and home is more remote than it was 10 or 20 or 40 years ago? If so, why?

How have state-mandated testing programs affected student-teacher relationships? Has an increased emphasis on improving achievement scores resulted in decreased emphasis on understanding children? Has there been a decline in the trust parents have in teacher and administrators making decisions that are in the best interest of their children? Why? These kinds of questions must be addressed in order to respond to the needs of at-risk students. The data in this study suggest that many educators do not actually know who is at risk or who is likely to become at risk.

The research accomplished over the years and the data generated in this study about retaining students in grade also highlight the issue about research and professionalism. Many teachers and administrators in this study thought that retaining students in grade was effective. However, research has consistently found that, without special intervention strategies, retention generally is not effective in terms of higher achievement or increased motivation. Can educators ignore such research because their own values or personal experiences lead them to believe otherwise? Is it appropriate and professional for educators to make decisions that are generally harmful to individuals and always costly to society in the face of such research? If use of research is an ethical principle for professionals, then should not educational practice reflect research?

Physicians try to adhere to the Hippocratic principle of "first, do no harm." Evidence in this study suggests that the idea behind such a principle is not always adhered to by educators. Education is not medicine, of course; but the general principle seems applicable as much to educators as to physicians. Is such a principle being ignored? If so, why?

Sometimes research on an issue is not conclusive; it is conclusive on the subject of retaining students in grade. Research on retention in grade is like research regarding smoking: almost nothing about either practice is positive in human terms. In some instances, retaining students in grade may not be detrimental if the student is given special help and a different set of experiences. But the evidence is overwhelming that retention, as it is usually employed, generally blunts students' enthusiasm, diminishes their interest in learning, increases the likelihood of their dropping out of school, and makes them feel badly about themselves. Thus if student learning is the basic purpose of schools, retaining students in grade appears to be unprofessional, unethical behavior. It violates the best information available today. The problem demands further study.

Do teachers and administrators know what the research says about individual differences or retention (Smith 1988)? Do they know what the research says about students who are at risk? About teaching at-risk students? If they do, do they accept the findings as valid and useful? Is their own teaching and administrative behavior influenced by the results? If not, why not? What kinds of information or experience would enable them to accept the findings? What do teacher training institutions teach prospective teachers about such issues? Do teachers learn about ethics and professionalism in preservice or inservice programs? Do they learn about the role of research in decision making? How do they learn it? How effective are those teachings? Who is responsible for helping practicing professionals acquire such learning?

Chapter Six
Simultaneous Replication

This chapter describes a way of doing research that is different from conventional approaches. It is called "simultaneous replication."

"Simultaneous replication" refers to a situation in which researchers at different sites study the same problem in the same way at the same time. In the study described in this report, researchers in 87 different communities used the same definitions, the same procedures, the same instruments, and collected data according to the same timeline. Finally, data were analyzed in the same way. In other words, the same study was repeated 87 times.

Replication is an important concept in the history and theory of science. To replicate in science means to do the study again, the way it was done before. Replication is important because it is the main way scientists verify research results. If a scientist reports findings that other scientists cannot verify when they replicate the study, the original findings are questioned. If a scientist reports a study, however, and if other scientists use the same definitions, procedures, and design and get the same results, then the results in the first study are supported and people have confidence in the results.

Simultaneous replication means repetition of a research design several times within the same time period. Simultaneity is not as important as replication; but added to the idea of replication, it enhances the credibility of the process by eliminating that which sometimes contaminates research results — variations across time.

Replication is also important because it guarantees accountability. If a researcher misrepresents the facts or even lies, that person will be found out when the study is replicated. Replication requires precise duplication of methods, instruments, and timelines. That kind of precision is relatively easy to achieve in the physical sciences; it is more difficult in the social sciences and education.

Important as replication is in the field of science, it is seldom practiced in education research because it is difficult to achieve. Researchers seldom use exactly the same instruments or procedures or timelines that other researchers use. Instead, they usually modify instruments or procedures or timelines to fit circumstances unique to their situation. Subsequent researchers usually try to improve what the first researcher did, but the variations in practice always mean that true replication does not occur.

Researchers in education generally try to design studies as carefully as they can, then trust that a number of studies on the same problem will "add up" over time, even though the various studies were done in different ways. Meta-analysis is one procedure that has been developed to achieve verification or substantiation of results without replication. Meta-analysis is an important methodological technique, but it is not replication.

Simultaneous replication is possible and practical when conceived and conducted within an organizational framework that includes centralized and decentralized governance units, which can expedite communication and coordinate activities. School districts and professional, business, military, or religious organizations could engage in research that uses simultaneous replication as a methodology.

Organizations that want to use simultaneous replication would find the technique most effective if they had sub-units that are separated geographically, a central headquarters with communication and dissemination capabilities, agreement on the common purpose of the organization, and a commitment to use research as one way to attain the purpose.

One aspect of simultaneous replication is especially attractive to people at the local level: it allows those people to be affected by local rather than state or national data. Simultaneous replication enables people at the local level to make the most of their own data, rather than be influenced by data that have been aggregated and summarized for a larger population. The following kinds of comments do not arise: "Those data do not apply to our schools. We are different. Our situation is unique." Simultaneous replication gives people control over their own data, its use and interpretation.

The general model followed in the Phi Delta Kappa Study of Students at Risk to accomplish simultaneous replication is well known; it has long been used for standardized achievement testing. Over the years, test publishers have developed instruments, manuals, and experience that allow educators to assess students' academic achievement in widely separated geographic settings. Those publishers have standardized testing instruments, instructions, time limits, scoring, and interpretation procedures. These standardized procedures make it possible for educators to have confidence in the results that achievement testing produces. In this sense, different schools that use the same standardized test to assess their students' achievement actually engage in simultaneous replication, but they seldom view it that way.

Because the testing instruments developed by the major publishers usually are developed with great care, are reliable, and include explicit procedures for administering the instruments, most people have confidence in the results of such testing. Uniformity, explicitness, reliability, and standardization are the keys.

Those who assumed responsibility for conceptualizing and coordinating the Phi Delta Kappa Study of Students at Risk accepted these characteristics of standardized testing as important qualities to be achieved in data collection and data analysis for this project. From the start, uniformity, explicitness, reliability, and standardization were assumed to be important to the success of the project. Everything was done to achieve those goals.

Accomplishing simultaneous replication by standardizing instruments and procedures was achieved in three ways: a manual was prepared, volunteer participants were trained to collect data, and data were analyzed in uniform ways. In addition, participants were trained to interpret the data that were collected in their local schools and to accomplish statistical analyses of those data. Each of these points is described as a factor that made simultaneous replication possible in this project.

The Manual of Instructions

A manual was developed by the research coordinating committee during the spring and summer of 1988 (see Chapter Two). The manual was 140 pages long. It was explicit. Every participating chapter used the same manual. The manual served as a standardizing element — the common denominator — in this research project.

The manual was divided into 13 parts. Each part was labeled a "job." Each job consisted of several "tasks" that had to be accomplished in a particular sequence in order for each job to be completed. Each task specified exact procedures, timelines, ways to cope with difficulties that might arise, and precise procedures for recording information.

After the first draft of the manual was developed, the data-collection portions of it were field tested in one school. Following that, major modifications were made. The manual was then duplicated, assembled in three-ring binders, and mailed to participating chapters one month before the three-day training session.

Training Participants

Participants met for three days of training in an isolated motel near the Kansas City airport. The manual served as textbook for the training. Each participant spent at least one hour in a small-group setting receiving instructions that pertained to each job. The instructions about each job were presented by the person who had primary responsibility for developing that portion of the manual. Discussions centered on the exact wording of the manual, what the terms meant, what to do in the event of difficulty, and the like.

At the end of the training, minor changes were made in the manual as a result of what had been learned during the training sessions. Each proposed change was discussed at length by the members of the research coordinating committee. The agreed-on changes were then presented to all participants at a general session, and participants recorded the changes line-by-line in their own manuals. The next week, copies of pages that had been changed were mailed to each participating chapter.

The manual served as a "constant" throughout this study. Following the explicit instructions in the manual, researchers collected data in 276 schools in 87 communities between 10 October and 15 December 1988. Researchers used identical definitions and procedures, and data were recorded in identical ways, according to the instructions in the manual.

Analyzing Data in Common Ways

Most of the data collected in this study were recorded in numeric form. Some of the verbal or other kinds of data (for example, case studies that included videotapes and narratives) were handled by the rules of qualitative research.

All principal interviews were coded by one person according to a protocol that included explicit criteria and detailed instructions about how to handle responses to each question. Following that, all data were recorded on computer disks.

Teacher Survey response forms were scanned optically. The resultant data were recorded on computer tapes.

Student Information data forms were completed by chapter researchers who recorded information provided by teachers who knew each student best. Those forms were scanned optically, and the data were recorded on computer tapes.

Data about holding power for each high school were summarized by chapter researchers on a summary sheet and mailed to Phi Delta Kappa Headquarters, where the data were entered onto a computer spreadsheet.

All data recorded on computer tapes or disks were organized according to an 80-column format, with the number of lines for each record specified according to the information to be included at that point in the data file. All data files were chapter-level (local) files. Finally, every data file was visually scanned to verify that appropriate information was recorded in the appropriate columns and that each record included the appropriate number of lines.

For purposes of simultaneous replication, data were analyzed with SPSS/PC + by preparing one computer program, then analyzing the data from each chapter with that same program, one chapter at a time, on the same computer. In all, 87 separate analyses were accomplished for each problem that was identified.

As of this writing, five problems have been studied by simultaneous replication: the relationship of class size with problems in teaching, the relationship of self-esteem with home and school factors, the relationship of locus of control with problems in teaching, the relationship of locus of control with class size and number of students failed, and the relationship of locus of control with class size by educational level.

In the first replication (class size and problems), five statistical computations were done for each of the 87 data sets, resulting in 435 values whose statistical significance was determined in conventional ways. Only 31 of the values were found to be statistically significant, thus the general hypothesis was not supported. Simultaneous replication did not confirm the general hypothesis that teachers who have smaller classes report fewer problems in teaching.

In the second replication (self-esteem and home and school factors), four statistical computations were accomplished for each of the 87 data sets; but when missing data were taken into consideration, only 79 data sets included enough cases (30 or more) to ensure confidence. Statistical computations for each of those 79 data sets produced 316 values whose statistical significance was determined in conventional ways. A total of 253 of the 316 values were statistically significant, and all in the direction hypothesized. And in 60 of the 79 replications, at least three of the four values were statistically significant. The general hypothesis was repeatedly supported that there was a positive relationship between a student's sense of self-esteem and father's occupational level, mother's educational level, achievement scores in reading, and grades received in school. Simultaneous replication confirmed the results.

The other replications produced mixed results. All replications involved studies using the data collected in the Phi Delta Kappa Study of Students at Risk, but those replications that have been done thus far were not studies of students at risk, per se. Each problem was selected because it was interesting in its own right, and because it was manageable enough to be tested by the simultaneous replication methodology. The fifth replication involved 276 analyses of data sets, that is, one from each of 276 schools rather than one from each of 87 chapters.

Knowledgeable researchers critiqued the above analyses; and on the basis of questions they raised, each problem was restudied, using statistical techniques and control variables in addition to those originally employed. Reports of these analyses are available as technical reports.

The Second Training Session

During March and April 1989, researchers from participating chapters met in small groups at seven regional meetings around the United States to discuss the aggregated data sets and to learn how to analyze their local data.

These sessions, conducted by the project director and at least one other person from the research coordinating committee, introduced participants to the limitations of the study, problems that had been identified with using the "At Risk Scale" scores, general summaries of the aggregated data, and an introduction to simultaneous replication as a research technique.

Following that, participants were instructed in how to verify their own data sets, how to use SPSS/PC + to analyze their data, and how to ask important questions of their data.

Using Volunteers to Collect Data

Phi Delta Kappa is a professional organization. Members regularly contribute their time, their money, their energy, and their talent to further the purposes of the organization: promoting quality education through leadership, service, and research. Chapter Seven describes how many people and how much time was contributed by members of Phi Delta Kappa to ensure the completion of this project.

Volunteers made this project possible. Volunteers accepted responsibility for the project in their chapter area. Volunteers spent three days in training, learning how to accomplish each of the 13 jobs. Volunteers collected data in the schools according to the instructions in the manual. Volunteers spent three additional days in training devoted to data interpretation and data manipulation. Volunteers made the project possible from beginning to end. All volunteers were professional educators.

Professionals generally are paid for what they do, but members of professional organizations often contribute to those organizations in different ways. Contributions made this whole project possible, and it was those contributions that made simultaneous replication possible.

Professionals who contributed their expertise to the project made it possible to collect data in schools in widely separated regions of the United States in uniform ways. Standardization of instruments, standardization of time, and standardization of data collection procedures meant that simultaneous replication as an idea could be fully realized. Once the data were collected, they could be analyzed on one computer quickly, one chapter at a time.

This last point — analysis of all data by one person at one place — is a deviation from the idea of replication as generally practiced in science. That is, even though the same problem was studied in different communities, if one person analyzed the data for the various communities, that one person might err, deliberately or unknowingly. In that way, the confidence that generally accrues to research findings as a result of independent replication was not ensured.

To guard against such a possibility, researchers at 19 chapters of Phi Delta Kappa received all of the data sets from all of the chapters. Those researchers were encouraged to analyze the data sets in whatever ways seemed appropriate and reasonable to them.

In summary, replication is important in science. The idea of simultaneous replication was tested as a methodology in the Phi Delta Kappa Study of Students at Risk by subjecting data that were collected in common ways with common instruments in 87 separate sites and subjected to common analytical procedures. The process works. Future reports will describe the procedures and results in more detail.

Chapter Seven
Evaluating the Project

This project was monitored and evaluated in four ways: regular reports to Phi Delta Kappa's Executive Director and the Board of Directors, review of activities by the research coordinating committee members, a brief summative evaluation of the main features of the Kansas City training session, and a summative evaluation of the entire project by participants in May 1989. Only the last two evaluative efforts will be described in this chapter.

Evaluation of Training Session

During the last hour of the training session in Kansas City, participants were asked to respond to six aspects of the training program on a five-point scale with 1 indicating "extremely negative" feelings and 5 indicating "extremely positive" feelings. Responses were recorded anonymously by participants on an optical scan answer blank. Mean response values for the 100 respondents are described in Table 2 on the next page.

These data suggest that the 100 participants felt positive about the training sessions in Kansas City; the meetings were worthwhile.

Final Evaluation by Participating Chapters

In early May 1989, after the last of the seven regional follow-up meetings, a six-page evaluation form was mailed to the local project director of each participating chapter. By June 15, responses had been

Table 2.
Mean Response of Participants to Items
About Training at Kansas City Meeting
(N = 100)

Item	Topic	Mean
1.	clarity of presentations	4.08
2.	opportunity to raise clarifying questions	4.60
3.	responses received to questions asked	3.97
4.	understanding the intent of the project	4.34
5.	understanding the design of the project	3.94
6.	creating team spirit and project ownership	4.11
	Overall	4.17

received from 61 of the 87 chapters that completed data collection on time.

The timing of the mailing was awkward, since most participants received the forms during the final days of the school year. However, it would have been inappropriate to distribute the forms earlier, because the last district-level meeting with participating chapters ended on May 1.

The evaluation instrument asked participating chapters to provide both factual data (for example, "How many people served on your local research committee?") and estimated data (for example, "Estimate how many hours you worked to coordinate this project in your area"). Participants were also asked to indicate their perceptions of the quality, significance, and worthwhileness of various aspects of the project on a five-point scale, with 1 being low or negative and 5 being high or positive. Unless indicated otherwise, the data reported here are averages.

On the average, 10 people served on each local chapter research committee and 14 other people assisted that committee in collecting data. A total of 238 hours were spent by the people in each chapter on the various tasks required to accomplish this project, while the person who chaired the local group estimated that he or she spent approximately 54 hours coordinating the activities of the group. Extrapolating from the data provided by 61 respondents to the 87 chapters that completed data collection on time, approximately 2,016 Kappans and others participated in this project, contributing about 20,700 hours working on various data collection tasks.

In all, 93% of the chapters indicated that they had enough time to respond to the original request to participate in the project. Further, 83% indicated they made presentations about the project at a local chapter meeting in 1988-89; and 90% indicated they plan to make such a presentation in 1989-90.

Extrapolating from the data provided by 61 respondents to the 87 chapters that provided data by the deadline, 122 persons became new members of Phi Delta Kappa as a result of participating in this project; none became irritated about the way the project was conducted and dropped their membership.

More than 20 research papers and other articles for publication had been prepared by chapter participants by 15 June 1989, and 12 dissertations based on the data collected in this project were scheduled to be completed by August 1989.

Asked to evaluate the training provided in Kansas City and the *Manual of Instructions* that served as a guide for this project, participants responded as follows:

Arrangements and facilities for the training	3.9
Job 1, Form a Research Committee	4.2
Job 2, Select Three Schools	4.1
Job 3, Prepare to Do the Study	4.2
Job 4, Interview the Principal	4.4
Job 5, Survey the Teachers	4.3
Job 6, Apply the "Holding Power Statistic"	4.3
Job 7, Write a Narrative Report	3.9
Job 8, Collect Information About Students	3.8
Job 9, Do a Case Study	3.4
Job 10, Do an Optional Project	3.6
Job 11, Do Further Analyses of the Data	3.7
Job 12, Interpret the Data at District Meetings	3.6
Job 13, Disseminate the Results	3.6
Assistance you got from Headquarters	4.5

In evaluating the information and experience provided at the district-level, follow-up meetings held during spring 1989 and the materials received since those meetings, participants responded as follows:

Arrangements and facilities for follow-up session	4.4
Printouts that described local student data	3.8
Printouts that described local teacher data	3.7
Computer disk that included local data	3.8
Computer disk containing programs to run data	3.7
Summary data about students from all chapters	3.8

Summary data about teachers from all chapters	3.8
Summary data about principals from all chapters	3.9
Summary data for "Holding Power Statistic"	4.1
Instructions for interpreting "At Risk Scale"	3.9
Instructions on how to use SPSS/PC+ on the microcomputer	3.6
Instructions on asking the right research questions	3.7
Instructions about writing for publication	4.2
Instructions on interpreting data on local disk	4.0
Manual of instructions on interpreting data	3.8

Asked to evaluate the project in terms of previous expectations (1 = "less than expected" and 5 = "more than expected"), local project directors responded as follows:

Time required to complete the project	4.0
Satisfaction gained from involvement	3.9
Learning acquired from participation	3.6
Consistency with purposes of Phi Delta Kappa	4.1
Benefits gained in terms of time and money spent	3.7
Estimate impact of project on the profession	3.6
Estimate impact of project on your chapter	3.5
Estimate impact of project on PDK as a whole	3.7
Estimate impact of project on your community	3.0

Local project directors evaluated various aspects of the endeavor as follows:

Way problem was identified by delegates	4.2
Problem studied	4.6
Design of the study	3.8
Methodology of the study	3.8
Results of the study	3.9
Time line followed	3.7
Opportunity for chapters to participate	4.7
Opportunity for PDK members to participate	4.6
Quality of the experience for those involved	4.3

The responses of participants to various items on the evaluation form were consistently high; they were positive about the whole experience. One of the 48 items received a mean rating of 3.0, the hypothetical mid-point, but the remaining 47 items had mean ratings higher than that, and 18 of the 48 items were rated 4.0 or above.

On the last page of the evaluation instrument, participants were asked to make additional comments about their involvement in the project. Some of the comments were positive:

> This has been a wonderful experience, and I pray that it is not left to wither on the vine.

> In my six years in southeast Kansas, this project has gotten more educators interested in research and the research process than any other single endeavor.

> I believe the study will prove to be one of the exceptional pieces of research conducted in this decade.

> This project was a first. I am happy to say PDK was finally doing the research part of our pledge.

Some of the comments were negative:

> When the results were returned, I was extremely frustrated and disappointed, for a lay person cannot understand the results.

> I think the project was too ambitious. We couldn't even get paid contractors to do the yeoman jobs we were asked to do in this research.

> There wasn't enough of a definition of "at riskness" at the start to enable us to justify asking schools to contribute all their time and space.

All of the comments were helpful. Detailed comments by all of the representatives of participating chapters who responded to the final evaluation form are included in Appendix C.

The proposal to the Board of Directors had outlined a project that was designed to do two things: 1) generate good data about issues; and 2) generate enthusiasm, participation, and a sense of accomplishment in research among Phi Delta Kappa members in up to 100 chapters.

The information provided in this report suggests that both goals were achieved. Some of the data collected in the study have been reported here, but the final report — to be published in the near future — will include extended descriptions of all data collected, most of which has not been included here. A careful study of the evaluation data emphasizes the fact that enthusiasm was generated, participation was genuine, and a sense of accomplishment did occur among hundreds of Kappans in 87 chapters. Both goals were realized.

Suppose we apply a cost/benefit rationale to this research project. What were the costs? What were the benefits? The Phi Delta Kappa Board of Directors authorized expenditures of $71,000 for the project, and each of the 100 participating chapters agreed to commit

$300 to be involved. In a formal sense, $101,000 was available for project purposes. But other monies were expended in the sense that people who worked on the project were paid by their own universities or school districts, and other costs were incurred by Phi Delta Kappa.

In the paragraphs below, these contributions have been assigned cost values based on certain assumptions. One assumption was that each participant's time was valued at $15 per hour (that approximates the hourly rate of a person making $30,000 per year). A second assumption was that teachers who responded to the survey instrument took about one hour to complete the survey. Numbers in parentheses represent costs contributed "in kind" (that is, paid for by the institutions to which people were assigned, not cash-out-of-pocket). The hours that people worked are based on data provided by chapter representatives as detailed in this chapter.

The following costs were paid by Phi Delta Kappa Headquarters during the two years of the project:

($100,000) for salaries of project director, secretary, others.
$71,000 for air travel, printing, scoring, etc.
$10,000 for editing and printing reports.
($6,000) for salaries paid by school districts that released members of the research coordinating committee to plan and coordinate the project (400 hours at $15 per hour).

The following costs were paid by local chapters of Phi Delta Kappa and by school districts and universities that provided released time for participants to collect data (20,000 hours at $15 per hour):

($300,000) for salaries of those allowed released time to collect data.
$30,000 for hotel and meal costs paid for by chapters.

($150,000) for the salaries of those who provided data were paid by local school districts that made it possible for teachers and principals to complete surveys and interviews (10,000 hours at $15 per hour).

Using these figures as estimates of actual total costs, this project cost $667,000 to accomplish, of which $101,000 was formally authorized and expended specifically for the project by Phi Delta Kappa. Another $100,000 was provided by Phi Delta Kappa in the form of salaries for people involved.

Each dollar provided by Phi Delta Kappa generated more than three dollars by other institutions. With 100 chapters participating, Phi Delta Kappa's costs of $200,000 (includes all expenditures) amounted to $2,000 per chapter during the two-year project. For each $2,000 expended, 22 people (on the average) worked more than 10 hours each on various aspects of the project (about $9 per hour for data collection). Out of the original $71,250 authorized, $33,000 was for participants' travel expenses; that represents a major portion of the total allocation (46%) provided directly to chapters rather than for administrative or other costs.

New knowledge was produced. Excitement and involvement for hundreds of people resulted from the study. The commitment to research — long stated as important for members of Phi Delta Kappa — was made apparent. Understandings were developed. Skills were refined. Collaborative relationships between universities and public schools were established. Research reports were written. Dissertations were completed. A sense of great satisfaction and accomplishment was expressed. But there was frustration and apprehension, too.

Are those things worth $667,000? Are they worth the $200,000 that Phi Delta Kappa expended on the project? The answer to such questions must be interpreted in the context of James Thurber's oft-quoted remark: "Compared to what?"

The project was not a revenue-producing project. Few funds will accrue to Phi Delta Kappa because the project was accomplished. If viewed as "service to chapters," the $200,000 resulted in hundreds of Kappans in almost 100 chapters working with thousands of educators in hundreds of schools.

In summary, participants were generally positive. They thought the project dealt with an important problem, was in keeping with Phi Delta Kappa's stated mission, brought people together in significant ways, was conducted in a professional manner, generated useful information, and highlighted problems that were only dimly perceived before the project began.

References

Anderson, Robert, and Ritscher, Cynthia. "Pupil Progress." In *Encyclopedia of Educational Research*, edited by Robert L. Ebel. New York: Macmillan, 1969.

Cogan, Morris L. "Toward a Theory of Profession." *Harvard Educational Review* 23 (Winter 1953): 33-50.

Frymier, Jack, et al. *Manual of Instructions*. Bloomington, Ind.: Phi Delta Kappa, 1988.

Grissom, J.B., and Shepard, L.A. "Repeating and Dropping Out of School." In *Flunking Grades: Research and Policies on Retention*, edited by Lorrie A. Shepard and Mary Lee Smith. London: Falmer Press, 1988.

Hodgkinson, Harold L. *All One System: Demographics of Education — Kindergarten Through Graduate School*. Washington, D.C.: Institute for Educational Leadership, 1985.

Holmes, C. Thomas. "Grade Level Retention Effects: A Meta-Analysis of Research Studies." In *Flunking Grades: Research and Policies on Retention*, edited by Lorrie A. Shepard and Mary Lee Smith. London: Falmer Press, 1988.

Holmes, C. Thomas, and Matthews, Kenneth M. "The Effects of Nonpromotion on Elementary and Junior High School Pupils: A Meta-Analysis." *Review of Educational Research* 54 (Summer 1984): 225-36.

Levin, Henry M. "Financing the Education of At-Risk Students." *Educational Evaluation and Policy Analysis* 11 (Spring 1989): 47-60.

National Education Association Research Division. *Estimates of School Statistics, 1988-1989*. Washington, D.C., 1989.

Otto, Henry J., and Estes, Dwain M. "Accelerated and Retarded Progress." In *Encyclopedia of Educational Research*, edited by Chester W. Harris. New York: Macmillan, 1960.

Pallas, Aaron M.; Natriello, Gary; and McDill, Edward L. "The Changing Nature of the Disadvantaged Population: Current Dimensions and Future Trends." *Educational Researcher* 18 (June-July 1989): 16-22.

Parsons, Talcott. "The Professions and Social Structure." *Social Forces* 17 (May 1939): 457-67.

Selden, Ramsay W. "Missing Data: A Progress Report from the States." *Phi Delta Kappan* 69 (March 1988): 492-94.

Shepard, Lorrie A., and Smith, Mary Lee, eds. *Flunking Grades: Research and Policies on Retention.* London: Falmer Press, 1988.

Smith, Mary Lee. "Teachers' Beliefs About Retention." In *Flunking Grades: Research and Policies on Retention*, edited by Lorrie A. Shepard and Mary Lee Smith. London: Falmer Press, 1988.

Unstattd, J.G., and Thornton, Robert D. "Secondary Education: Student Population." In *Encyclopedia of Educational Research*, edited by Chester W. Harris. New York: Macmillan, 1960.

Vollmer, Howard M., and Mills, Donald L. *Professionalization.* Englewood Cliffs, N.J.: Prentice Hall, 1966.

Appendix A
Areas Included in Study

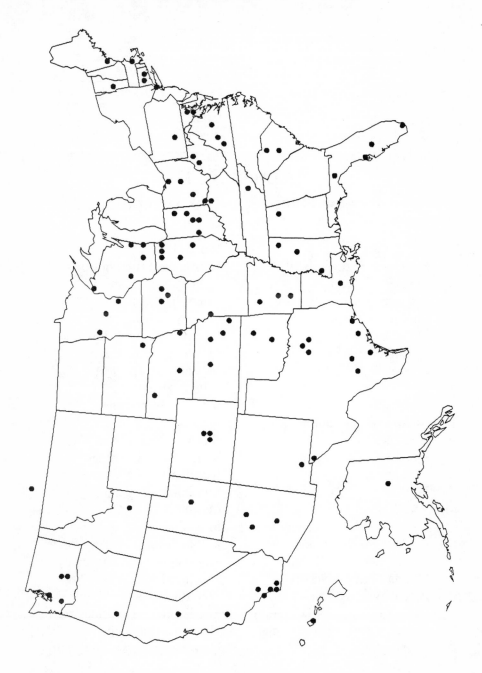

Appendix B
Chapters Participating in the Study

Ball State University
Beaumont Texas
Bradley University
Brigham Young University
Burlington Vermont
Butler University
Central Nebraska
Central Washington
Clearwater-St. Petersburg
   Florida
College of St. Thomas
   Minnesota
East Central Oklahoma
   University
East San Diego County
   California
Emporia State University
Farthest North Alaska
Florida Southern College
Florida State University
Fort Wayne Indiana
George Washington University
Greater Cleveland Ohio Inter-
   University

Harvard
Henderson State University
High Plains Colorado
Huntsville Alabama
Idaho State University
Imperial Valley California
Indiana State University
Indiana University of
   Pennsylvania
Indianapolis Indiana
Iowa State University
Kanawha Valley West Virginia
Kansas State University
Kenosha-Racine Wisconsin
Lynchburg Virginia
Marion Area of Ohio
Mid Cities/UTA
Mid-Willamette Valley Oregon
Mississippi State University
Moorhead Minnesota-Fargo
   North Dakota
Mt. St. Helens Washington
Natchez Mississippi
New Mexico State University

Northeast Mississippi
Northern Illinois University
Northern Kentucky Area
Oklahoma State University
Pasadena California
Phoenix North Valley
Piedmont Area South Carolina
Pittsburg State University
Quad City Iowa/Illinois
Radford Virginia
Rainier Area Washington
Red Cedar Area Wisconsin
Red Deer Area Alberta
Sacramento California
Saint Cloud State University
San Antonio Texas
Sheboygan Wisconsin
Sinnissippi Illinois
Smoky Valley Kansas
South Carolina State College
Southern Arkansas
Southern Connecticut State
  University
Towson University
University of Arkansas
University of California/Los
  Angeles

University of Cincinnati
University of Dayton
University of Denver
University of Hawaii
University of Houston/Clear
  Lake City
University of Illinois
University of Missouri/Kansas
  City
University of Nebraska/Omaha
University of North Texas/
  Texas Woman's University
University of Northern Iowa
University of Southern Maine
University of Tennessee
University of Texas/El Paso
University of Virginia
University of Wisconsin/
  Superior
Victoria Texas Area
West Virginia University
Western Nebraska
Whitewater Wisconsin
Yakima Valley Washington
Yavapai Arizona

Appendix C
Comments by Participants

On the last page of the evaluation instrument, participants were asked to write about their involvement in the project. The specific instructions follow:

> On this page, please write a paragraph or so describing your perception of this project, including the problems you have encountered and the accomplishments you have achieved. Try to share what the project has meant to you and your colleagues — positively or negatively — and the kind of impact it has made (or will make) on your chapter in the months ahead. What did you learn the most about? What was the most fun? What irritated you most? What do you wish you could do differently if you had a chance to do it over? Use anecdotes, illustrations, or whatever might help to communicate the totality of the experience for you and those who have been most directly involved.

On the pages that follow, comments by participants are quoted in their entirety and exactly as they were written on the evaluation form, but they are anonymous. Each paragraph represents the comments of one person.

This was an important and challenging undertaking; the topic was timely, and the baseline data it has provided will be of great value to educators and those interested in the problem of students at risk. The project gave a great "boost" to our local chapters, and the ripple effect will be felt well into next year. I expect several new members will be inducted into our local chapter as a result of the activity and interest generated by this study. The manual set forth quite well the significance and scope of the project. It was explicit about the importance of astute selection of members for the research committee. How fortunate we were to have: recently retired superintendent, the Uni-Serve Director for the surrounding school divisions, the personnel director of one of the larger rural school divisions, a director of a private day-care center, a principal, a faculty member involved in institutional research, and two faculty members involved in teacher education. We felt exhilarated upon completion of the task. It was necessary to assign and sub-divide the jobs, putting one member of the committee in charge. The definite timeline drove us − that was important. The notion that this was a prestigious organization for which we were providing data inspired us to do as careful and thorough a job as we were capable of doing. It became necessary to make some judgments about what information we could reasonably expect to get on the student op-scan sheets. I believe the holding power formula and the data gathered will be of great interest to area high schools. I would hope that it, or one like it, becomes standard for the nation so that statistics are meaningful. Dr. _____, co-director of the project, and Dr. _____, a member of the research committee, are analyzing data according to the proposal they submitted. We are looking forward to hearing from them about their findings. Dr. _____ has suggested that we let other faculty at this institution and those at _____ and _____ know about the study and data collected and let them help in the analysis. There is much that can be done with what has been gathered, and it should prove useful as baseline data for future studies. The Appalachia Educational Laboratory is involved in the national Rural Small Schools Project, and I anticipate sharing with them what we have accomplished. This has been a stimulating experience for me and for those on the committee with me.

I enjoyed the project, but would have revised the questionnaire. Too much of the data collected was perceptual rather than factual. I enjoyed interacting with the participants from across the U.S.

This has been such an exciting project for me. It has made obvious certain strengths and weaknesses. The most striking weakness is how really little we honestly know about the students who sit in class every day. The gaps in our information were absolutely appalling. We know very little about too many students other than date of birth, biological parentage, immunization and other health records, academic performance, and address. Parenthetically, maybe we lost more than we knew with the discontinuation of the old Smith-Hughes teaching certificate which necessitated home visits made to each student each year by teachers with that certification. Another eye-opener was the difference in preparation for the principal interview. Two of the three principals had virtually completed the copy taken to their school about two weeks previously. Those interviews went "smooth as silk." One principal, however, misplaced the first copy, which I replaced. The replacement copy was also misplaced. At the time of the re-scheduled interview, he was given his third copy. Neither did he really listen to two rather lengthy explanations given earlier about the nature of the research. It was disillusioning, to say the least. But the counselors, occupational specialist, and registrar in that school were extremely helpful, even providing donuts and coffee for several days. Teacher cooperation was fantastic. I do not recall a single "grumpy" teacher. One made the remark, "This took a lot longer than I expected." To this I replied, "I feel that way about it, too." Fall is always a busy, busy time, and I agreed not to ask the schools to gather data to which my office has access. My three secretaries did a yeoman's job in collecting basic enrollment data on participating students at each of the three schools in the project. The "Holding Power Statistic" is such a positive way of looking at an old problem. This concept has been very favorably received. This summer we will be trying to incorporate significant portions of this study into our "regular" work. The usefulness of projects is never fully realized until the work becomes indigenous. This is our goal. I want to thank you for having confidence in our chapter. Not everything was on time, but most were! We consider ourselves one of the 87 participating chapters.

This has been a wonderful experience, and I pray that it is not left to wither on the vine. The quality of the program, the research format, the development, etc. is unquestionably superb. The only real hang-up was framed in two areas — time and personnel. Working schools and school districts simply do not have personnel available to screen records, to interview teachers, etc. The few counselors and administrative personnel who made themselves available to work on the pick-and-shovel jobs inherent in the program did so because of the very nature of the program. Faced with testing requirements in the school's programs, most counselors and staff agreed to assist on the program as time became available. Teacher attitudes varied with the schools. Where teacher morale was high, willingness to tackle extra projects was offered less belligerently. Where morale was less ebullient, cooperation was more grudging. The true professionals came through under any circumstances. Since I intend to retire at the end of this school year, I intend to donate my time personally to following up on this project to make sure that my efforts and the efforts of my colleagues are not wasted. What a disaster, to have all that beautiful data and then let it sit! How tragic! My chapter has supported me to the hilt on the performance of this project, even to presenting me with the PDK Service Key. There have been words of praise, encouragement, and all kinds of kudos. I can't escape the feeling that, "Boy, am I glad you're doing this and not me!" Not too many offers of help have come my way — none, to be exact. Nevertheless, through this project, the raw data to pinpoint the most serious problems confronting education are sitting on our collective desks. If PDK doesn't live up to its leadership role and scream to the high heavens for the education community to wake up and get moving on meaningful programs, then no amount of money can salvage a once proud and dedicated profession. We've got the data. Now, let's use it.

Due to the teachers' work slow-down in _____, it was felt that most of the important data was unobtainable, therefore we were unable to make any significant conclusions regarding our study. We were also hampered by the time limitation. We did learn, however, that it was difficult to obtain data from the schools.

In terms of scope and ambition, this was an incredible undertaking. It stretched the capabilities of our group — both in terms of time and expertise — to the limit. It has made an impact by involving the chapter in research, which is an oft-neglected area. In retrospect, I wish we had involved more chapter members. The actual involvement of the chapter as a whole was too limited. The financial expense was great — over $1,000. There is some frustration over the "usefulness" of the results. Specifically, what do we have to take back to our districts, schools, and members? I believe that we have contributed significantly to the knowledge base, and this is worthwhile. Massive research, though, generates conclusions slowly, and some are asking for practitioner-user findings. This is a difficult order to fill. The most rewarding aspect of the project was getting into the schools. The resultant interaction was great. Most frustrating were the time pressures — two years would have been better. Please keep us informed of analysis activity.

People are ready and willing to volunteer time and efforts on what is perceived to be a worthy endeavor. We learned how fragmented and uncooperative the various agencies are that deal with at-risk children, and how those children can manipulate these agencies (school, home, social services, juvenile authorities, including the court system). Going into the schools, working on site, was the most fun. Most irritating were the less than adequate research design and limited feedback on findings of the study by International Headquarters staff, and lack of cooperation by a county human services department. If we were *ever* to do such a project over again, we would need a much clearer statement of what would be involved (time, effort, cost, personnel, etc.) before making a decision to participate. The letter you sent to chapters in 1988 asking them to apply for participation did not come close to a definitive statement of what would be involved. Second, a more rigorously tested research design and methodology would be required. The lack of testing instruments in this study for validity and reliability was unconscionable. Finally, we would not want to be involved in a study again that was driven by Jack Frymier's political agenda — to quickly do a study so a report can be given to the Biennial Council. It seemed that much of the sloppiness of this study was due to the "pressure" to have some findings for the meeting of the next Biennial Council; therefore, we all rushed through it from start to finish.

I was most irritated by not having the computer program to work on the data. In fact, it is blocking what I need to do. I was upset that you lumped two high schools together and I can't report accurately. That is really getting me depressed. The most fun was being part of what I believe is *the* most significant study ever done — not for the results, but for the methodology. I loved working with Jack and Bill in the small groups. What was so great is that we all can recognize that this was a first. I liked talking with the other people; it helped me grow. The part you should have seen was my case study. I laughed at how nervous my camera crew became as we headed for the prison. We were all frisked and then relaxed as we finally got to work. The case study work was the most rewarding because it put a face on what "at risk" means to the individuals. I have a greater personal commitment to the students I work with every day. I have reconfirmed what the business of teaching is all about — building human beings, one child at a time. I hope this will continue to be my feeling. I have so much appreciation for you after this experience. Words fail to describe my internal reaction. Should you plan to do another one of these, I would love to help in any way I could.

An interesting project in the evolution of research in PDK. Many problems for us [in that our chapter] doesn't have an academic nucleus of researchers like some chapters. Ours does better for recruitment and membership enhancement with service projects. There was modest individual value in our chapter setting. Collectively and socially, the emphasis on this issue can lead to motivation to do more in the community. Schools alone with diluted authority can do little to correct at-risk behavior. As a former Department of Army survey analyst, I think the project was too ambitious. We couldn't even get paid contractors to do the yeoman jobs we were asked to do in this scenario. Also, too many people handled the data to have the highest degree of integrity. We can look at this as a mammoth pilot study, but it will take more definitive and better controlled efforts to achieve great validity. I think it will take a network of designated research (high quality) chapters to attempt a similar project. I temporarily sacrificed my own job assignments and health to do my share, and I don't know if I can recover what I voluntarily gave up. While I am dedicated and interested in the project, nothing about it was fun on this end. I think the project was designed too quickly and from the point of view of someone who had authority over the data collectors, without being sure that such data really existed or in the amount requested. The joke was probably that I felt like a frustrated graduate student who could only withdraw or fail, without really knowing if what I was doing could be judged as acceptable. At times it was making research instead of conducting it. More attention can be given to data collection instruments. The "shotgun" approach is a little unwieldly. If it were my project, I would organize a network of about 30 "high test" university-affiliated chapters and obtain a designated sample of schools and chapters with an explicit data collection and sampling plan to support refined research objectives. Two or three of the university "cells" could subcontract for a fee to do the hard analysis and writing. At-risk behavior, like disease, is too comprehensive, and it needs a strategy for classifying at-risk behavior, with various analysis protocols for resolution (diagnosis/treatment). I would not recommend our chapter to do this again due to our loose structure.

The subject is one I feel very strongly about! I believe the study will prove to be one of the exceptional pieces of research conducted in this decade. Much enthusiasm was garnered. Much interest generated. PDK was exemplary in the professional and businesslike way in which the study was handled. I'm thrilled with the study and so pleased to participate.

A good project. The questions and procedures could have been a little better prepared if the printing of materials had occurred after the Kansas City meeting and after the chapters had opportunities to ask questions.

Chapter participation in the PDK national research project on at-risk kids has been by far the most exciting and professionally rewarding experience I have enjoyed since becoming a member of PDK. The study will undoubtedly start ongoing, local research projects (as intended) designed to shed light on local problems. If this can be accomplished and becomes standard operating procedure for our profession, I can think of no greater contribution that the project could make, not even the conclusions from the data collected on at-risk students. The interaction with colleagues in area public schools and within our university was a source of great satisfaction for all participants. The fact that we were helping collect data for a national study was another source of pride for all who participated. Many times, small local groups and individuals in rural areas feel insignificant and powerless to have an impact on the "big picture" in education. This project has done wonders for our local chapter members' pride and credibility with the communities involved. If we can capitalize on the receptiveness by providing even *one* positive contribution to schools in this area as a direct result of this participation in the project, then a door will be open that would have been much tougher to open by local initiative alone. There is currently a great working relationship between the university PDK members and public school PDK members and with area schools and the local PDK chapter. We are already discussing problems requiring research which can assist teachers to empower themselves to offer their own solutions to education problems rather than being jerked this way and that by state mandates. The implications are highly significant and critical in this time of educational change. If, in fact, significant structural change in education is occurring or is about to occur, then the arming of teachers with research skills and habits is crucial to the improvement of teacher credibility, which is essential if increased teacher empowerment is to occur. As coordinator of the project for our chapter, I learned a great deal and profited from my association with Dr. Frymier and other PDK staffers, as well as other project participants. On the local level, I found the case study was the most interesting aspect of the project for me. It breathed life into the national statistics, although it was sad and frustrating that we were not in a position to help our subject, who is desperately in need of intensive, professional attention. We became so immersed in the saga of our case study that we ignored your deadlines for completion of the job (as I'm sure you are well aware), but we are committed to finishing the job shortly. The written case study will be completed this summer, and the tape should be edited and pieced together before September 1. Thanks for your great inspiration and persistence to tackle such a project, and for your excellent guidance throughout, despite health problems. This project has been a significant professional catalyst for me and for our chapter.

Limited timeline (shortness), kinds of questions asked on student survey for high school cohort, limited direction and understanding of time needed to complete case study, description of conducting Holding Power Statistic could be improved by providing clear example. Principal interview too long in detail.

Overall, I think the project was important and beneficial for PDK and our chapter. The schools involved got a lot out of it − just from the aspect of collecting data and thinking about students in ways they don't traditionally think about kids. Some teachers/staff were ticked off because they perceived they were not "included" in the decisions to participate. This was a problem caused by lack of communication. In one school, teachers were expressly involved from start to finish because the principal had a style that required it. This is where we had our most success. I did feel that at the Kansas City meeting many questions arose or glitches were discovered that should have been spotted prior to the study's launching. In an effort to get things under way it seems the team overlooked things that needed to be considered: more pilot testing of instruments would have been helpful.

Our major hindrance was that our members were not available during the school day to collect data, so all information about students was collected by me. Also, the schools were 20-40 miles away, so travel time was a factor. The last session with teachers was cancelled for snow, so much middle school data was missing. The high school was 10-12, so 9th-grade data was difficult to obtain. The major benefit was contact with other professionals — local, national, and district. Also, I hope to publish and speak on related topics. Although I did most of the data collection, chapter members felt involved in providing data at their schools, and several are interested in interpretation.

Above all else, for me one of the significant outcomes was the opportunity to interact with others who are interested in educational research, whatever level of professional involvement. It became a superb group and provided the rank-and-file members [with an opportunity] to interact with Kappan leaders. Your motivation, inspiration, and ability to interact in a significant and pleasant manner was quite extraordinary. An important learning outcome, and one I am discovering myself in a survey project, is the difficulty of wording survey questions to incorporate all possible contingencies. In order to deal with this, should PDK do another project such as this, I suggest a preliminary design-development meeting in districts before the instruments are finalized. I thought the Kansas City meeting drove that point home.

When the invitation came from PDK International announcing the opportunity to participate in the research project, "A Study of Students at Risk" with 99 other PDK chapters, I was thrilled and strongly encouraged our chapter to "answer the call." The project was represented as "the greatest research project ever to be attempted" and our chapter wanted to be included. So, we applied, were accepted, and completed our part of the program. The first, and probably the greatest, disappointment we encountered was the reject from our prime choices of schools in the area. We had to settle for the schools that would allow us to come in and gather information. These schools were good schools, but we did not feel they were truly representative of the area. The schools that permitted us to use their information were not the schools that had the most students at risk. However, they were the best representatives we could get. We were disappointed in the instrument used to gather information about the students. There were so many questions that could not be answered because the information was not available. This was extremely frustrating and led to feelings of guilt and inadequacy. We also felt that the large number of unanswered questions weaken the validity of the research. What did we learn the most about? As yet, we have not learned anything about at-risk students that we didn't already know. However, we learned that members of the chapter can be extremely cooperative when there is something challenging to do. What was the most fun? The training session in Kansas City and working with the chapter members. Kansas City was well-organized, informative, and time well spent. I could not go to the session in the spring, but was told by the person who represented our chapter that she felt guilty spending the chapter's money because "we really didn't do that much." Our chapter chose

71

not to work on raw data. Therefore, we may not be reaping the benefits from this project that others are experiencing. Hopefully, the chapter benefits from this project are yet to come. If the impact of this research is as great as we were told it would be, our chapter, with all the other PDK chapters, will be bursting with pride because of our contribution.

The project gave our chapter a constructive, cohesive focus for the year. It brought several members "out of the woodwork" and brought nearly 15 new members into the chapter. It has created numerous contacts for continued collaboration between university faculty and public school teachers and administrators. We are now called upon for help because this project showed we could provide relevance to school needs. Schools have begun to gather information about children and families based on Job 8. Guidance counselors are changing record-keeping systems to have better information about kids. Teachers are asking how much and how come they know/don't know about their pupils. Our major problem was getting parental permission to do a Child Study. Superintendents don't have a great deal of confidence in teachers keeping confidentialities so they backed out on parts of the study.

This has been a good experience. I especially enjoyed seeing the people from the different districts and the university working together so effectively.

In general, I thought that the study was a positive and worthwhile experience. The support given by Jack Frymier and his staff was tremendous. The design of the study with respect to explicit directions was well done. I found the limitations of the project to be in the timeline set by PDK directors. My research committee found it very difficult to meet many of the deadlines, given the magnitude of the data to be collected. I also found problems associated with sorting out the data. The conditions of the disks we received from PDK was poor (the tape which we received was inaccurate). In closing, my recommendation would be for clarity regarding the way the data should be analyzed. All national data must be presented accurately if we are to do an analysis at the local level. Could PDK consider writing a SPSS/PC + program for analysis of raw data? It doesn't appear to be such a great task, and it would conserve the time of 100 chapters in writing 100 separate programs.

Several positives are easily identified: this was a very relevant topic for our school districts; this was a splendid opportunity for a field chapter to participate in an authentic research project on a national level; Neville Robertson's process for determining the list of at-risk factors was a learning experience in itself; we learned that research is tedious and that facts are difficult to find; the most fun was working with our enthusiastic research committee and deciding "ignorance is bliss." Unlike our college colleagues, we are not grounded in research, hence we followed all the jobs without difficulty and met time lines easily. A disappointment: our case study. We hoped for a more thorough investigation, but the school ran into problems with gaining permission for visits and taping.

One of the positive aspects of this project was that the steering committee included individuals in varied areas and levels of education. Public school and higher education administrators, counselors of higher education and public school faculty and graduate students worked together in planning, implementing, and evaluating the project. It was frustrating to find out that the case study would not be completed. One committee member had made arrangements for this part of the project to be completed close to the close of the project. Unfortunately, the student moved from the school district prior to the interviews. In retrospect, the case study should have been planned for completion before the closing weeks of the project.

There were many positive aspects resulting from our chapter's participation in this nationwide research project on at-risk students. The project generated data on a very timely and important topic, both nationally and locally. The project was a success here because the individual members of the research committee and the four agencies comprising the consortium made the commitment to work together. More than 35 persons contributed time to this research effort. This project provided new members for PDK, and it gave the chapter an opportunity to do research. It gave local schools the tools to use in development of and in enhancing at-risk programs, the videotape, and the local versus national profiles. The project gave members an opportunity to interact with people across the country and the PDK staff. The major negative aspect was the number of tasks that needed to be accomplished in the time frame provided. Everyone on the research committee already was working full time. Some suggestions are as follows: 1) Design future studies so that the local chapters can draw a random or representative sample so that the data will be more generalizable and, therefore, more useful to the local school teachers, principals, guidance counselors, and central office staff. However, this means that PDK will need more time for the tasks involved in the study. 2) Better timing when working with local schools and their calendars is a must if current data is needed, as it was in this at-risk study. 3) Recommend the idea of using a consortium involving local school district personnel as an effective model for conducting similar research projects. Chapters can leverage more ownership in the research project, and this may ensure that research results will be used by those who can make a difference. Other benefits to the local chapter: Each member of the research committee was provided copies of notebooks and PDK materials, such as a research manual. Local school district's director of research has discussed intentions to replicate portions of the study during the coming school year using a random sample. Plans for dissemination include presenting at superintendents' conferences and at a statewide department of education conference, publishing articles in the chapter's newsletter, presentation at a PDK chapter meeting next year after further data analysis has been conducted by the research committee, dissemination of PDK articles to regional audiences via regional newsletters, Lab/Center Network, etc. The committee plans to continue its work throughout the next year to analyze data. Local district has already held several meetings to share data with at-risk coordinators' group and the three schools involved in the study.

The project was accepted well by most participants. Our chapter paid teachers for their time to collect the data; this may have relieved some of the anticipated resistance. There was concern by all data collectors regarding the accuracy of the student information. This type of project is extremely valuable to all participants and, as a model, could surface important information to the teaching community. I think it could have been made a better project if 1) chapters had been involved in the design, and 2) a pilot study was completed prior to the questionnaires being finalized.

Positive Aspects: Working together for a common goal brought a sense of purpose to our chapter. Teachers and principals came to see themselves as researchers and able to gather data systematically. Simply meeting deadlines on top of full-time jobs was a major accomplishment. The rough results received confirmed our own instincts of what places our students at risk. We were surprised at the test data across three diverse districts, each 30-40 miles apart. Negative Aspects: the high school people felt very pressured for time, and could not get enough time to do the extra students to offset the two smaller populations at grades 4 and 7. The project was costly for the chapter, because we paid for substitutes for the teachers in gathering data about students. Districts provided Kappans released time, but they were not happy about it due to tight budgets. The chapter feels its members will not participate in future endeavors. Time, costs, and results did not make it significant at local level, though it's realized it will have a significance nationally.

The two high schools were particularly interested in the Holding Power Statistic. I did this part of the research study and was able to locate a number of students who had previously been identified as dropouts. This brought their percentages of "locatable" students up. They were pleased. Our chapter (only 5 years old) was excited about being selected as one of the participants. It helped our chapter's "self esteem." Working with Dr. Frymier and the other team members was a "growing" experience for me. They are highly organized, so knowledgeable, and a great group to work with! Thanks for the opportunity.

The project brought our chapter together to work hard on a research project — an activity very appropriate for PDK. Members became more excited about the chapter, and we established very positive relationships with our schools. We had a wonderful evening of recognition and celebration for the total group involved in the study. As the superintendent of a small district, I am so totally committed to my job at this time of year (spring) that I have not been able to devote the time needed for reporting, dissemination, etc. In mid-June when school ends, I plan to "catch up." Our case study had such a dramatic turn of events and positive ending that the person who wrote it feels it was an extremely significant experience. We all enjoyed the project — working full time in a public school, however, seems to make the project more difficult than if we were on a university professor's schedule.

Participating in this project has been most rewarding. I appreciate the caliber of expertise and leadership provided by the PDK staff at the Kansas City and Dallas meetings. Their advice and ideas on tackling this project were most helpful. I sincerely hope that the data generated in this study will provide help for educators throughout the United States to not only identify but learn ways to help our "at-risk" students remain in school.

Problems: short time frame from Kansas City meeting until data due at PDK; little time to study and analyze data (local problem). Accomplishments: first major research project for our local chapter; one participating school changed its database as a result of the project; one participating school is considering a longitudinal student study as a result of the project. Enjoyable Parts: our optional study of interviews with students in special "anti-dropout" programs provided a chance for one-to-one conversations with some interesting young people. Do Differently: for a study of this magnitude, a pilot study and chance to validate the instruments would seem worthwhile.

The project has awakened the educational community to direct attention to which students are at risk and to think about what they can do or should find out to assist students in being successful. The educator Kappans in this area are highly interested in a real sense of the "unknown" in regards to how to marshall efforts to "combat" the problem. Educators are seeking a direction in meeting the needs of today's students, and many feel a lack of direction and frustration. I would make some changes in the instrumentation, particularly the student instrument. Since my orientation is to the research area — all the activities were fun (to an extent), but looking at the data and making meaning of it is probably the most exciting part of the project. Many renewed contacts were made during the study with teachers and students. Several non-Kappans asked how an individual becomes a member of the organization.

I enjoyed working on the project. I particularly enjoyed interacting with other coordinators in Kansas City. That helped me more than anything else.

Would suggest that videotaping problem — students in a large urban area — is most difficult because of the many permissions needed.

Our information on the student survey was very incomplete because school records did not contain the required information. It was very difficult to find school staff who could give *accurate* answers about those personal areas. Staff probably gave the most honest and complete answers to any survey we have ever presented to them. We have been working with "high risk" dropouts for the past 15 years in our alternative high school. We have been very successful in identifying these students early in their school life, but we still have a lot of difficulty with 1) developing positive self-concepts, 2) having positive and effective communication with the home, 3) encouraging staff to work more effectively with these students.

Although I love involvement in research, I did not enjoy involvement in this particular project. I was inspired at Kansas City, but once I carefully studied and delved into the project, it soon became apparent that the tasks (jobs) were greatly involved and some impossible to do completely (gathering student data). Teachers and administrators soon became reluctant to assist, and some were down right rude. In short, the jobs were impossible to do by people who work all day. This project was too time-consuming and too detailed, as well as too much of an undertaking. It would be better in the future to break up such a large project into smaller ones. When the results were returned, I was extremely frustrated and disappointed, for a lay person cannot understand the results. Why couldn't someone use simple wording to express the results — maybe some visuals. I felt my time was mostly for nothing. No administrator has time to study the results and implement new programs.

The study has served as a vehicle to focus educators on the problem of "at risk." During teacher interviews and when gleaning student files for at-risk factors, all involved became very aware of the combination of factors that can affect students. The camaraderie with local chapter members and with members from other chapters has been especially rewarding. Mutual interest in research topics among members has prompted further collaboration across the country. The realization that we were all collecting data for a single important study brought strength and insight to all. On the downside, the analysis of local data is at a standstill. Members don't have the insight, knowledge, time, or direction to pursue what is seen as an enormous task. Collecting data had structure, direction, and a definite time frame. Analyzing the data, posing significant questions, and providing meaningful information to schools and decision-makers seems overwhelming. We expected more analysis and direction from the PDK study group.

Please kindly help by providing our two participating school districts with a separate teacher data run. Bruce already helped with the students. Please consider that the local district summed data is as important to these schools as the national study. Also, I think [our state] should have been distinct from North America from an academic standpoint. We appreciate all efforts by Bruce, Neville, and Jack in helping resolve this.

The Study of Students at Risk addressed significant and timely issues and afforded PDK members from the community, school, and university sectors opportunities to work collaboratively toward important and well articulated goals. Our chapter members spent long hours of committed service in completion of the project. As such, the Chapter Research Committee certainly would have appreciated more direct, consistent, and immediate feedback from the national project directors. For example, our chapter completed Jobs 1-8 and submitted all necessary data a full two weeks prior to the scheduled deadline. Unfortunately, we received no recognition or even confirmation that the data had been received by the national committee. When depending on volunteers for completion of a project of the magnitude of the Study of Students at Risk, it is imperative that participants are promptly and appropriately recognized for their commitment and service. Note: We still as yet have not received confirmation of receipt of our videotape and case study.

Positive — Has aroused a great deal of interest in "at-risk" notion. Questions about early identification of students — elementary grades — seems important so that early intervention can occur. Many are ready for the next step: What can we do to help "at-risk" persons. Negative — I'm concerned that some educators had to be treated to hard-sell tactics to get them involved. I did not take "No" or "I don't think we can do this" responses with regards to efforts such as this project.

We haven't finished yet! We are still transferring data from the computer printouts to more useful forms. The end is not even near!

I felt that this was a highlight of my professional lifetime. It gave me a wonderful sense of teamwork with Kappans around the country. People here saw that PDK is directly involved in research that would help children and youth with reduced learning.

The students-at-risk project was time-consuming but rewarding. As a result of this research, three members with excellent expertise became fiscal, again. Their interest had waned, and this project ignited their enthusiasm. As the group reported the findings at the final PDK meeting, the members of the research committee beamed with pride about their accomplishments. The part I liked best about the research was the method by which "at-riskness" was operationalized, giving a score. I will be able to suggest this technique to doctoral students. Another plus is the information available for publication. Although not available yet, the chapter's last issue of the newsletter highlights the research. Time for the activities was the biggest negative factor. Some of the deadlines were difficult to meet.

Allow me to discuss the bad news first. Lost one team member because of a perception of project requiring too much work. Individual was mature enough to suffer in silence, so it did not affect the remainder of the team. Holding Power Statistic incorrectly calculated — numbers of students rather than actual students were tracked — this will be corrected by the end of May. Required case study (10th-grader) not completed — youngster was suspended, then quit school and dropped out of sight. Hopefully, the optional case study being completed on a middle school youngster will take up the slack. And, now the good news. In my six years in southeast [state], this project has gotten more educators interested in research and the research process than any other single endeavor. "Ink" devoted to this project has given area educators real courage of conviction. A number of district and regional level projects and task forces have been initiated to study the "at-risk" student. Has afforded more visibility to an already visible chapter of PDK. Meeting attendance has increased about 20% since the announcement of our involvement in the project. Has served as a real "ice-breaker" for conversation between Kappans in this part of the world. Old and new Kappans have a starting point for initiating or renewing friendships. The research team worked so well together in their sister institutions that visitations, swaps, and cross-district inservice meetings are being discussed. Has gone a long way to reduce the inequalities that are many times perceived between university and public folks. In sum, it was the right activity on the right topic at the right time. I envision at least a couple of years of research and development on at-risk students in this part of the world.

It was frustrating not to be able to get in on the ground floor of the development of the study. Our high school student data was provided directly by students. The at-risk factors appear to be more present than in the general study. I am suspect of the validity of the national student data. Schools do not have good data about students.

There has been great enthusiasm among the school people who participated in this project. We will be making presentations of the data to the chapter and the involved schools early in the next school year. We have just started to analyze our chapter data and the national data. We separated the pieces of the project into three parts. Two of the three teams functioned well and completed their tasks on time. The third team did all their work at the last minute, putting great strain on the successful meeting of PDK timetable. All in all, everyone involved has found the project worth the considerable time and effort required.

This was an exciting project that allowed our chapter to experience a "real" research study. It permitted teachers and administrators to join in a collaborative endeavor and demonstrated to us that our districts are very supportive. The prestige of PDK and the fact that many top-level administrators in all three cooperating districts are members was also a critical factor in their willingness to collaborate. We experienced frustration in trying to find answers to questions about individual students and coping with situations in which there was non-documented information about student or family problems that could not be reported. The student information gathering was by far the most difficult and time-consuming part of the project. The impact of this project has not yet been felt in our districts, since it was not possible to get officials together for a reporting session. This will be done in August or early September. We will also be reporting at our area superintendent's roundtable and to our PDK chapter as a whole. The greatest difficulty was encountered in completing student information and coordinating all aspects to complete the data gathering by the December deadline. One of our key district researchers also suffered a heart attack and was unable to complete the holding power statistic, so that fouled up our whole schedule.

The project was most worthwhile. I was extremely pleased to see PDK involved in research of this nature. I would hope we could do more like it. The participating school personnel gained a significant awareness of the problems associated with at-risk students. Also, the fact that school records are seriously lacking in important information about all students and that if the school is to be a vital force in helping the at-risk student, more information must be available to teachers and counselors. Meeting with the school personnel was very rewarding to me personally. The concern for at-risk students is there, but many schools do not know what to do or how to do it. This project did much to improve this situation. While doing Job 9, the case study, it was interesting to note that the attendance of the student being studied improved because she wanted to see the person doing the study. She enjoyed the attention, and the teachers reported a positive change in her behavior as a result of the study. I believe the school has taken a renewed interest in this student, and she may not become another at-risk statistic. The results of the project have not, as yet, been reported to our chapter nor feedback given to the schools. This feedback and reporting will take place early this fall, and our committee looks forward to meeting with the schools. The project has provided the opportunity for the faculty of our counseling area at the university to become better informed about the at-risk student, and we are preparing our counseling students in their role with these students. All in all, the project has been very beneficial.

I was particularly pleased with the level of involvement from chapter members who helped with data collection at our three sites. Because we are located in a university community, we also had the benefit of involving graduate education students in the project (several of whom were non-members). Although the amount of data to be collected was immense (given the time frame), the cooperative spirit of both data gatherers and school personnel at the three sites was gratifying. My concern now is with making sense of the data and reporting results to school officials and teachers — data that I hope will be useful for their purposes.

Our experience was one of surprise that the project was so haphazardly designed and overlapping/repetitious/sprawling. There wasn't enough of a definition of "at riskness" at the start to enable us to justify asking schools to contribute all their time and space. Parts were unrelated to other parts: teacher perceptions of what works for at-risk kids, then asking about parental/familial suicide. I think the teacher and principal information and the case studies will prove most valuable and all the student data least valuable because it is so unfocused. We enjoyed doing it, and our schools were cooperative, but we really have nothing to give back to those schools that will help them.

I have been impressed with the project: the topic, the effort made by you and your people in the design and methodology of the study, and plans for future studies. I enjoyed getting better acquainted with area educators. I also feel that our chapter leaders feel a need for some project to generate interest. Future projects will work, provided time is taken to obtain understanding with participants.

This project was a first. I am happy to say PDK was finally doing the research part of our pledge. We have spent a lot of time talking and eating. I am quite aware of all the egos that were involved in this project, and the team at Kansas City handled this well. This project allowed me to see some talent in our chapter. They worked very well! I do not feel these first steps were anything but great. The hardest part is putting it together in a meaningful way for our chapter. Any problem gathering the data was really insignificant. It was a pleasure working with Jack Frymier and an outstanding team.

I personally found the project to be a very positive experience; for the most part I have always been interested in research and have long felt that we do not do enough of it in the public schools. Or private schools, for that matter. I learned a lot working at the local level, and also from my attendance at the Kansas City and regional meetings. It was nice to learn that our chapter was not the only one which was struggling at times with certain issues. I found the PDK central committee to be very supportive, understanding, and encouraging. Locally, I believe our chapter gained from being involved in an endeavor such as this. It made the research part of PDK become much more real. PDK became better known out in the schools of the area. Local members of the committee got involved in PDK activities which they had not been before. One very active member of the local committee had noted on a questionnaire that his schedule did not allow at-

80

tendance at many of the usual meetings, but that he was interested in research, if that opportunity should ever present itself. He got involved in a very large way. So, too, did another member of the university staff. Thus university personnel worked closely with public school people on the committee — administrators, teachers, school psychologists. It was a nice blend. Right now I am struggling with what we have in terms of data gathered from the work. I hope that this becomes clearer as I and others locally study what we have, so we can present this in a meaningful and logical way to the other members of the chapter, the school staffs involved, and perhaps others. Right now I feel somewhat hanging. Perhaps that is because I/we have not had time to look over the data received closely enough. Yesterday one of our committee members, one of the university people and a computer expert, took much of the data forward to peruse. He and I plan to get together in a couple of weeks to compare notes. Yesterday we had a chapter meeting which was well attended. I presented to the group, walking them through the project to this point. It seemed well received. A number commented on the intensity of the project for those on the committee. If I had known before the regional meetings what I know now, I would have brought along another member of the committee, one well versed in computers. I did find this questionnaire hard to respond to. That is why it is coming in late. I picked it up several times to work on some of it, set it down, then started again. I hope the information provided is helpful. It did force me to pull together some information in a way I would not have otherwise, I guess.

The project has had a very positive impact on our chapter. Members have been more enthusiastic and involved in this project than any I have observed. We received a district grant to complete part of the project. I believe the success we experienced will lead to more coordinated research within our chapter. I hope it will lead to further national efforts. The major problem I found was the data collection. The data tape of the national data shows problems in entering and verification of the data. Also, in the future, the planning of the statistical analysis needs more thought in advance.

This project came along at the right time for us. We were attempting to increase our research focus, and this gave us a perfect vehicle to accomplish our goal. We have gotten participation from some members who have not been very active as well as those who are always there. The holding power statistic (well over 80%) was a surprise to us, since the high school selected was 90% Mexican-American and mainly low-income. This was helpful in supporting current efforts to help keep the students in school. Thanks again for a great experience!